Anonymous Heroes

Martin Daley

HAYLOFT

First published by Hayloft 2009

Hayloft Publishing Ltd, South Stainmore,
Kirkby Stephen, Cumbria, CA17 4DJ

tel: 017683 42300
email: books@hayloft.eu
web: www.hayloft.eu

ISBN 1 904524 73 7

CAP data for this title are available from the British Library

Designed, printed and bound in the EU

Papers used by Hayloft are natural, recyclable products made from wood grown in
sustainable forest. The manufacturing processes conform to the environmental
regulations of the country of origin.

For Wendy

Sergeant 3741 James Curran, The Border Regiment

Contents

Acknowledgements   6
Introduction   7
PART 1: JIM CURRAN
    A Changing City   11
    One's place in the Empire   21
    The trouble with Alliances   29
    A quiet Sunday morning   38
    Gallipoli. Where?   46
    The best laid plans   54
    Nowhere is exempt   62
    The F word   72
    The Border lads   80
    No-one is exempt   88
    Postscript   93

PART II: WILLIE GRAHAM
    Enter the Black Sheep   96
    What is poverty?   106
    Suffering and Suffrage   113
    Call to Arms   121
    Ammunition and Alcohol   129
    Preparing for History   136
    Hey Lads Hey!   144
    Carnage   152
    One of life's survivors   160
    The end's in sight   168
    Postscript   177

Principal Sources   181

Acknowledgements

I would like to thank the following people and organisations for their help and support with this book.

My researcher George Smith provided sterling work and displayed his expertise in accessing individual records at the Public Records Office in Kew. My own mother, Noeline Daley and Great Uncle Freddie Graham provided invaluable anecdotal information about my own family's history.

The staff at the Carlisle Library and the County Records Office – to whom nothing was too much trouble – helped enormously as I trawled through seemingly endless records.

From a military point of view, Stuart Eastwood, curator of the Military Museum at Carlisle Castle helped enormously with his general enthusiasm, his providing of many photographs contained within the book and his knowledge of the Border Regiment during the Great War.

Speaking of photographs, I must make particular mention of Carlisle historian Ashley Kendall who allowed me access to and use of his wonderful photographic collection, including the poignant cover photograph of a recruiting march in Lowther Street, Carlisle, in late 1914. Other organisations who kindly allowed use of images were Tullie House Museum, Carlisle Library and the Imperial War Museum. Image credits have been printed alongside the caption for each picture – I hope they are all correct! (Apologies if not).

I also thank Dawn Robertson for her continued support of my work and her colleagues at Hayloft Publishing for the production of such an impressive book.

Introduction

ALL too often history is treated simply as a production time line of dates and facts: 1215 – the Magna Carta; 1642 – the beginning of the English Civil War; 1805 – the Battle of Trafalgar etcetera. And even when historians pause to look beyond the headlines, they invariably concentrate on the main characters immediately associated with the episode: King John, Oliver Cromwell or Lord Nelson. Rarely are the layers of history paired back sufficiently to highlight the lives of ordinary people like you and I.

One mammoth historical chapter dominates this book: The First World War. But let me stress immediately this is not intended to be a military history in a conventional sense; in fact, it is not intended to be a military history at all. This catastrophic event has sometimes been labelled, 'a family affair'; this is because virtually every royal house in Europe that took part in the conflict, descended in some form from Queen Victoria. When she died in 1901, she had over ninety living descendants scattered around Europe who were therefore not only connected to the British Royal Family, but also to each other. Disaster lay ahead for these great monarchies as – by the end of the war – Tsars, Kaisers and Emperors would all see their houses fall. But other families were also involved in the conflict: yours and mine – and it was with much less fanfare that our ancestors' ordinary lives were changed forever as Imperial autocrats' dynastic ambitions took precedence over the lives of their subjects.

Never in history had so many taken up arms; never had war reached so far beyond the battlefield and cut so deeply into the fabric of society. For millions of men from five continents, this was the defining moment of their lives – many of them would be sent to their deaths as the violent Twentieth Century was set in motion, and the endless rows of white gravestones in cemeteries dotted around the world remind us all of the scale of the carnage. And for millions of women left behind, the quality of their cruelly austere lives would be worsened (if it were possible) as they were left alone to shoulder the emotional and financial burden of the loss of the house's patriarch figure. The legacy of the ordinary man from this period is usually a few faded and chipped letters on a monument somewhere. But each one had a face, each one laughed and cried and lived a life under incredibly difficult circumstances. This book is predominantly about two of them.

Jim Curran and Willie Graham walked the same streets as I walk, visited the same places – cinemas, theatres, pubs – I visit, did the same everyday things I do. But they also did things I will never do (thank God). They served their country in foreign fields; they experienced the horrors of the trenches and the death and disease that went with it on an unimaginable scale.

Throughout this book, the 'A List' characters of the period like Lloyd George and Lord Kitchener get their usual look-in, but studying the past shouldn't just be about the big names and I am determined that characters like Jim Curran and Willie Graham should not be confined to the No Man's Land of history. The intention is that Jim and Willie receive parity with the great and the good; I have attempted to do this by piecing together civil and military records, and family anecdotes and letters, with the grand histories and events we may be more familiar with. These are two ordinary blokes who can be used to personify the millions of everyday men who took up arms for their country in 1914. They are also great grandfathers of mine.

When I was once talking to my own father about his national service experience, he came out with the modest phrase, '...we weren't proper soldiers really – we were just ordinary lads.' It struck me later that that is what all rank and file are: ordinary lads, from ordinary backgrounds; fallible, vulnerable and [significantly] plentiful. Men like these don't usually get a look-in, because most military and social history books tend to concentrate on the bigger strategic – sometimes global – issues, in the most detailed minutia. As excellent and enlightening as such conventional histories are, so many of them miss out on the human element of the story, simply referring to masses in terms of numbers (*"the British Army numbered 77,000 at Waterloo,"* or *"31,000 working class people died in the cholera epidemic of 1832"*) I want to buck this trend.

But then, how does one begin to unravel such a global event to focus on two everyday characters and their families? Those making the case against writing histories of such people will legitimately put forward the fact that there were simply too many of them – where could one possibly start? I have to concede that the stories of two men from one family can do scant justice to the millions that have served their country but if it makes only a few readers appreciate the pains of our forebears, the my efforts will have been worthwhile.

From a civilian point of view, the lead up to war was a seminal period for Britain, as the working classes showed the first signs of social and industrial unrest by demanding an end to Empire and equality for all. Many historical romanticists still view The Edwardians as a genteel group with a naiveté that today almost seems amusing; the whole Edwardian period is portrayed as one like one long, lazy, summer's afternoon in pastoral England, where everyone sits in an immaculately manicured garden, wearing Panama hats and white flouncy dresses, having tea and scones, while the sound of leather on willow can be heard on the nearby village green. Of course it was never like that for the majority of working class Britons who scrimped and scratched to make a living. How did national and international events affect them? What was the impact of the People's Budget of 1911? Did the introduction of the Labour Party and the increase in trade unionism have a positive influence on their existence? And how did a single gun shot, 2,000 miles away in an obscure Balkan state influence their destiny?

From a military point of view, recorded actions of individual servicemen are extremely rare (although the amount of information on Willie Graham in the Public Records Office is staggering – we shall see why later) and therefore when focusing on each individual; in most cases the movements and the actions involving his company or platoon tell of his adventures and the hardships he endured. In some cases, there is more information available on him during his civilian life; this takes us beyond his service number and brings the human element to the chronicle.

In doing so, I hope I can do justice to the individuals and their comrades, as, after the war, there appears to have been an unspoken conspiracy of silence amongst those who fought at the front, and then fought just as hard to suppress and forget what they had endured upon their return home; their memories cauterised and closed to the horrors. A classic example is Harry Patch, the last Tommy who didn't speak about his experiences until 1998 when he was 100 years old.

The book combines my interest in local, family, social, political and military history, and is intended to give enough coverage to the intricate international machinations that led the world towards catastrophe. But it is predominately about these local men. It is not intended to put their achievements and experiences – and those of the Border Regiment in which they both served – above, say the Lancastrians or the Anzacs at Gallipoli; or the Irish Regiments and Canadians on the Western Front. Nor is it intended to suggest that their home-lives were any harder than their contemporaries elsewhere in the country. It is a very partial view of the late Victorian and Edwardian period and through the brutality of the First World War – or the Great War as it was called until the second catastrophic event of the twentieth century dragged scores of countries around the globe into a second calamitous conflict.

War, slaughter, hardship and sorrow dominated the lives of our ancestors. As for Jim Curran and Willie Graham, they were no exception to this and – 90 years after the First World War – this is their fifteen minutes of fame.

Martin Daley, Carlisle, 2008

JIM CURRAN
1
A Changing City

AS these words are written, in the first decade of the 21st century, the city of Carlisle is witnessing yet another change to its cultural make-up. With the development of the European Union and the relaxing of its continental borders, the city – like the rest of Britain – is experiencing a large migration of mainland Europeans, keen to seek employment and make a better life for themselves, and their families back home. The less generous or welcoming amongst the populace send up the usual cry of 'they are only here to take our jobs and sponge off the authorities.' It all has echoes of the country throughout the nineteenth century when it wasn't Poles or Portuguese, but Scots and especially Irish immigrants who flocked to England in search of a better life; anything to escape the hardship of famine and unemployment in their homelands.

Carlisle had its fair share of numbers throughout the century: the early years saw the first boom in the Industrial Revolution and the textile industry provided thousands of jobs for the unskilled masses; individual chancers and family units flooded in to compete with one another for work and a roof.

One such family was the Currans from County Mayo. Patrick Curran was born in 1806 but he would be 39-years-old before he and his wife Mary (ten years his junior) made the decision to move to England. The year of their migration was 1846 and they brought with them their new-born son, James; but 1846 wasn't only significant because of James's birth, it was the year in which the worst famine in Irish (and European for that matter) history commenced.

The dilemma facing Patrick and Mary was stark: stay and suffer the almost inevitable consequences, or leave – probably never to return – and start a new life on the mainland. They chose the latter option and it proved a wise choice: over the next four years, Ireland would lose a quarter of its population – over a million people dying of starvation; the Currans home county of Mayo would see 30 per cent of its population perish.

Upon his arrival in Carlisle, Patrick – like so many of his countrymen – set up as a cotton weaver and secured a tenancy on a house in Annettwell Street opposite the castle. Although he and his family had escaped the horrors of Ireland, he was arriving in a city whose once burgeoning cotton industry was starting its decline and as times moved from the mid-to-late Victorian period, those captains of Carlisle's industry, Messrs Dixon and Ferguson were seeing their once mighty empires crumble. With this decline, the numbers of Celtic immigrants was reduced from a flood to a trickle, and by 1855 – although the odd drifter would try his luck in the Border City – the arrival of young families like the Currans, had virtually dried up altogether.

But then over the next fifteen years, the railways and new factories would see Carlisle re-emerge as an industrial centre, and the escalating jobs market again brought the inevitable influx of immigrants to follow in the footsteps of their forebears who had been attracted by the opportunities in cotton, after the Napoleonic Wars.

By 1870, the population topped 30,000 for the first time (the figure had trebled since the turn of the century). There was work aplenty with Hudson Scott opening its new factory on James Street in 1868 and Cowan & Sheldon moving into the city at St Nicholas Works a year later. In the four years that followed Isaac Teasdale would establish a factory and John Laing would start his building company.

These were changing times for the city's inhabitants, and with the increase in opportunity came the (albeit still limited) chance for many to have electoral representation. The Second Reform Act of 1867 gave the vote to many tenants and lodgers with a residential qualification of at least twelve months; in the General Election the following year, Carlisle increased its voters by 230 per cent.

And if the city had seen that one great taboo of politics change, then the other, that of religion – and particularly of religious tolerance – was unrecognisable from the early decades of the century. This was not surprising, given that most of the immigrants – including the Currans – were Roman Catholic.

Religious convictions had played a key – not to mention controversial – role in Carlisle's history up to this point. Parliamentarians and Royalists, Protestants and Catholics, English and Scots (and Germans) had all exchanged blows and fought for control of the city in the name of religion, during the bloody mish-mash that were the British Wars throughout the turbulent Stuart dynasty. Once the Jacobite Rebellion had finally been quelled in 1746, the government made the conciliatory move of encouraging Catholic highlanders to become members of the British Army, probably on the premise that it is wise to keep one's friends close, and one's enemies closer. And of course with the spectre of William, Duke (or Butcher!) of Cumberland looming large with his scorched earth policy, it is a safe bet that many clansmen felt it was an offer they couldn't refuse.

Increasingly in the years that followed Catholicism was brought into the mainstream and it culminated in the Catholic Toleration Act of 1791 which allowed Catholics to build chapels and places of worship. Seven years later, the first Catholic Chapel was built (on West Walls) in Carlisle since the time of the Reformation.

It was shortly after that, that one of Carlisle's unsung historical heroes appeared. His name was Joseph Marshall. The 33-year-old Yorkshire Reverend had been educated in Valladolid, Spain and after his ordination he was appointed by the Vicar Apostolic of the Northern District to establish a mission in Carlisle. He set about providing facilities for the steady flow of Irish Catholics that poured into the city in the first half of the nineteenth century, but also – in a sort of prototype Churches Together concept – worked to establish ecumenical links with other denominations.

When he arrived, there were little more than a few dozen in his congregation;

Green Market circa 1889 (courtesy of Carlisle Library)

by the time of his death in 1854, the number of Catholics in the city was in excess of 3,000. Reverend Marshall was also instrumental in building the city's first Catholic School: St Patrick's was opened in 1826 with facilities for 200 children of all denominations.

But much of the hard work done in Carlisle, and the small progressive steps for Catholicism throughout England almost came undone when – three years before Reverend Marshall's death – Pope Pius IX chose to make English prelate, Nicholas Wiseman a Cardinal and Archbishop of Westminster. This Catholic hierarchy was the first in England since the reign of Elizabeth I. Wiseman's first act stoked the fires of religious conflict in a pastoral letter, when he claimed that Catholics would seize the first opportunity to govern. Nationally, those who resented the expansion and upsurge in Catholicism sought to express their dissatisfaction with a vengeance. The Carlisle press quickly followed suit, criticising Wiseman, the Pope, and the Catholic religion in general. The *Journal* was initially (and appropriately) liberal in its criticism, acknowledging that religion was a matter of individual conscience (providing that was Protestant, of course) rather than by royal or governmental decree. The editor of the *Carlisle Patriot* however, had no time for such wishy-washy, fence-sitting, clap-trap:

> *Wiseman's defence of his position is crouching and hypocritical, hostile to the constitution of the country and insulting the clergy of the Established Church. People like Dr Newman are perverts, not converts.**

For weeks after, the local papers carried endless reports and published countless letters vilifying the Catholic religion. What must Joseph Marshall have thought in the final years of his life – all of his good work for naught? The rumpus caused by Wiseman's appointment certainly soured relations between Catholics and Protestants, both nationally and locally; for years to come, signs advertising job vacancies and available accommodation carrying the legend 'No Irish' (effectively meaning, 'No Catholics') became common place.

Still, there were those who persevered in breaking down such sectarian boundaries. In 1859 the Poor Law Board ruled that Catholic children in work-houses should not be instructed in Protestantism and priests were officially admitted to the workhouses to give Catholic instruction.

---

* John Henry Newman was seen as a controversial figure by many. An Anglican, in early life he was a major figure in the Oxford Movement to bring the Church of England back to its Catholic roots. Eventually his studies in history persuaded him to become a Roman Catholic in 1845. He was later made a cardinal.

And locally, Marshall was succeeded by another hard working visionary: Reverend Luke Curry was a champion of education and it was he who undertook to build a school and chapel in Caldewgate, in honour of the eighth century monk, the Venerable Bede, in 1868. Three years later, in October 1871, the first purpose-build Catholic primary school, named after Bede's contemporary, Cuthbert, was build on Union Street. Instantly, St Cuthbert's became the biggest Catholic school in the city with 350 children (St Bede's had 264, St Patrick's 179).

These opportunities in education came too late however for Patrick Curran's son James who, by the time of developments in organised schooling, was starting adulthood; and whereas he may have been free to openly practice his religion, finding work as an illiterate Catholic jobbing labourer could prove a little tricky if he found himself in competition with a born and bred Carlisle Protestant.

In 1870 James met and married fellow Irish immigrant Mary Nelson. The two had to make do with living with James's parents in Annettwell Street. If married life started inconveniently and frustratingly for 24-year-old James, it was soon to turn to tragedy when, twelve months after marrying, his wife Mary died trying to deliver their first child; the infant was also lost. Such tragedy was sadly commonplace amongst the lower classes of Victorian Britain, and was apparently accepted as a standard hardship of the working population. For his part, James dealt with his loss by living with his parents for a further two years before he met someone with whom he was destined to venture into married life once again.

Margaret McCue had her own hard-luck story by the time of their meeting (who didn't in those days?). Like James, she was another Irish Catholic immigrant; unlike James she did not appear to be receiving the same support from her parents in her time of need. The single, illiterate, 23-year-old power loom weaver had become pregnant in 1867; it is believed that her father John threw her out of the house in disgust, upon hearing the news. Thereafter she took up residence as a boarder with Catherine Butler at No. 4 Milbourne Street. In June 1868, her son Michael was born (the father is unknown) and in 1872, she met widower James Curran – the two married on 25 January 1873.

This may have been a rich time for the workers of the city in terms of choice, but in the context of gaining wealth that was quite another matter. James inevitably moved with his new wife and adopted son into to the affordable Irish quarter of Caldewgate, which saw thousands of workers and their families crammed into the tiny lanes, yards and courts that sprawled away from the main Bridge Street towards the river on one side, and neighbouring Shaddongate on the other.

Affordable it may have been but it would appear that many of the inhabitants of Caldewgate were as rough as the living conditions. Four years before the Currans' moved there, one reader of the *Carlisle Journal* complained of the ward's tenants in a forthright letter to the editor:

> *Sir, Permit me through your column to bring to the attention of the authorities, the disgraceful scenes that are taking place week after week in the neighbourhood of Caldewgate. It is no common thing to see drunken sots staggering from a few of the licensed houses in this locality, not only belching forth oaths and blasphemy of the most revolting description, but in the full blaze of the day, setting the rules of common decency in defiance. The police, it is said, are powerless in this matter, and to all appearances fail to find a remedy. It is surely monstrous to suppose that peaceably inclined persons are to be subjected to the scandalous annoyances and the law and its officers remain unable to cope with the evil... A number of rogues are in the habit of congregating on the footpath at the bridges and down as far as the square, and it is almost impossible for ladies to pass without being exposed to indecent remarks.*

Knowing what they were moving into, the young family settled down to

An open yard in Caldewgate circa 1904 (photograph courtesy of Ashley Kendall)

their tolerable, if austere life becoming tenants at No. 19 Cooperative Court, a one-up, one-down property. Such virtual slum-properties had burgeoned, with the constant flow of immigrants to the city; but with the overcrowding came the inevitable price of disease and premature deaths. A year after the Currans' marriage, W H Power produced his lengthily titled 'Report on the Local Government Board on Recent Epidemic Prevalence of Fever in Carlisle, and the Sanitary State of the City.' In it, he lamented:

Enteric fever is habitually present, to a greater or lesser extent, and was rather seriously prevalent during the first quarter of the present year. The more recent epidemic of fever has been typhus, probably at first imported, and spreading under circumstances of crowding and squalor, till it has attained the proportions of a severe epidemic.

Before the year was out, Margaret was expecting her first child with James, but when the time came, delight and tragedy fought for attention in the Curran household: a son, John, was born in May 1874, but amid Caldewgate's squalid atmosphere, Margaret's six-year-old son Michael contracted typhus – the very disease that had so concerned Power – and died two weeks later. Such heartbreak can only be imagined and it would be another three years before James and Margaret enjoyed the birth of their second child – a daughter they named Mary.

James may have just missed the chance of a good education but his children were ideally situated to benefit from the development of primary schooling. The great Education Act of 1870 had demanded mass elementary education, or at least literacy for all and brought Britain into line with its European neighbours. Throughout the continent, between 1870 and 1914, the numbers of primary school teachers multiplied; in Britain – which had no public education system before 1870 – it trebled. Living in Caldewgate, the Catholic children naturally went to St Bede's. Reading through the Log Book of 1877 gives a fascinating insight to the conditions and varied curriculum – and extra curricular activity – enjoyed by the children: subjects consisted of arithmetic, reading, writing (on slates), geography, history; there were lessons on trees, food, natural history and the solar system; and the forward thinking staff would develop the other skills in the children with singing, needlework and sporting activities; and special treats for the children were also in evidence for instance a conjuring performance was given by 'Professor Lennon' during the lead up to Christmas.

On 25 April 1879, another little Curran appeared at Cooperative Court,

Caldewgate. James, named after his father, swelled the numbers to five. James senior continued working as a general labourer, moving from job to job to bring home sufficient earnings to feed the children; from the factories to the railways, there was usually something available for a young, fit man. And if you fell out of regular employment, there was always the opportunity for seasonal work at the hirings.

The hirings provided employment on a half-yearly basis, at Whitsun (May) and Martinmas (November). Hundreds of men and women wanting work would flock to the Market Place, hoping to catch the eye of a prospective employer. If successful, the hirer would give the new found employee a sixpence (2.5p) or a shilling (5p) as 'earnest money' to confirm the appointment.

So if James's goal was to ensure employment, Margaret's was to ensure the children were healthy and fed regularly. Ironically, living on Cooperative Court, Margaret would do much of her shopping at the Cooperative stores, set up over a decade earlier to give low wage earners the chance to purchase affordable products. And then there were the street markets: market days were on Wednesdays and Saturdays, and the inhabitants of Caldewgate – being the Irish quarter – took advantage of the available poultry, eggs and pork at the unimaginatively named 'Paddy's Market'. At harvest time from 26 August, there was a continuous market known as the Great Fair which lasted for fifteen days and not only provided an opportunity to pick up the odd bargain, it gave some fairly light relief to the austere lifestyle of the impoverished Carliseans.

Young James was baptised at St Bede's on 15 July 1879, but tragically, the infant and his siblings were soon to experience the cruelty of the here-today-gone-tomorrow existence of the nineteenth century working classes. Shortly after his son's christening, James senior started feeling a little uncomfortable and a growth gradually appeared on his neck. Over the following months he became increasing ill and during July 1880 – with Margaret unable to look after him and the children – he moved back in with his parents, who by this time had moved out of the city and were living on California Road at Kingstown. But Patrick and Mary could do little for their son and on Monday 2 August 1880, he died of what was diagnosed as cancer. He was 34 – he had outlived his first wife by a mere nine years and left his second with three young children to raise.

Three days later, he was buried in a paupers' grave at Carlisle Cemetery. Dying is an expensive business today and in 1880, it was also emotionally and financially unforgiving for those left behind; pauper or not, Margaret had to pay double fees as James was a Roman Catholic and he was living in Caldewgate, technically outside the district of Carlisle.

What was Margaret to do? She was 33, Irish, illiterate, with three children under the age of ten to raise. She may have been illiterate but she wasn't stupid: on 1 March 1881, barely eight months after her husband's death, she married again. There was no such thing as a whirlwind romance amongst the needs-must poor of Victorian Britain; there was no time either for any nonsensical 'what will the neighbours think?' John Pollard had come north to the city from his home town of East Farndon, Northamptonshire, to work as a labourer on the west coast railway – he was 36. Upon marrying Margaret, he became step-father to her three children.

By the time young James had joined his brother and sister in attending school, St Bede's had its new school and chapel built on Silloth Street, where it would remain for the next 76 years. The Pollard/Curran family was by now

The hirings in Lowther Street in 1892 (photograph courtesy of Tullie House Museum & Art Gallery)

living in the part of Caldewgate that was known locally as 'Poet's Corner', as William Shakespeare, John Milton and Lord Byron all had streets named after them. Henderson Square was just off Byron Street (and immediately behind the Joiners' Arms that still stands today). Another family, living a few doors away was the Thompsons. William Thompson was an engine fitter from Scotland who, like so many, moved down to Carlisle with the second coming of the railways to the city. In 1880, he met and married Isabella Reed, from yet another Caldewgate family. William and Isabella had four children; the eldest of which, Mary Ann – named after her grandmother – was the same age as young James Curran. The two were among hundreds of children who played in the streets, making their own amusement with tins and hoops and anything else that would fuel their collective imaginations.

Like many of her kind, Isabella Thompson suffered a double tragedy within a couple of years: first her father, Jacob Reed, died leaving her mother – also Mary Ann – destitute. Isabella and William took her into their home but in February 1888, William himself was killed in a railway accident, leaving his 30-year-old widow to look after their four children, her own mother, and her sister Kate for good measure. The experiences of Isabella Thompson and Margaret Pollard (Curran) were remarkably similar therefore; equally their respective children, young James and Mary Ann had the tragedy of never really knowing their fathers.

2
One's Place in the Empire

THE late Victorian and Edwardian periods have been rightly noted by historians as being a period which had a profound effect on social and economic life in Britain. The internal combustion engine and the application of electric power radically altered transportation, while wireless and telegraphic cable would transform communications throughout the world. But too often, the innovation and achievement deflects attention from the poverty and adversity faced by millions of working class people.

It may be a cliché to suggest that once someone gets on the downward financial spiral it is almost impossible to arrest the slide; but then the opposite is also true: once one gets the snowball to success, it just gets bigger and bigger. Such was the case in latter years of the nineteenth century as the rich got richer and the poor had to make their own arrangements. Capitalism grew as big businesses and large enterprises developed at the expense of small-town, small-time operations. From 1880 on, the pattern of distribution was revolutionised; 'grocer' and 'butcher' now meant not simply a small shop keeper but increasingly a nationwide or international firm with hundreds of branches.

In 1800 Europe had a population of five million with only seventeen of its cities boasting a population of 100,000 or more. By 1890 that figure had shot up to 103 with a total continental population more than six times as large as that at the beginning of the century.

Carlisle's population had grown to almost 40,000 by this point, an amazing increase of 10,000 from 1870. By the middle of the 1890s, the diseased James Curran's two sons were now of working age and looking to get a foothold in this tough uncompromising world. Both young James and his elder brother John would go over the Caldew Bridge into Carlisle to find work at the hirings. Evidence of the difficult times in which these boys were growing up comes in the record that during this period, one third of the working population was unemployed and half of this number was also homeless. This was reflected in the numbers of desperate men and women attending the hirings that were regularly moved around the city centre – from the Market Place to

English Street, to Lowther Street – to accommodate the ever-increasing numbers. The boys obtained regular labouring jobs in the latter half of the decade, and at the Martinmas Hiring of 1897, held on Swifts Lane and Strand Road, James (now Jim in this adult world) secured a job as a Field Drainer earning fifteen shillings per week. (In 1901, at the request of the Cumberland Chamber of Agriculture, the Carlisle Town Council agreed that all future hirings should be held in the open space in front of the Town Hall).

Jim's lifelong friend Mary Ann Thompson meanwhile, was working as a tin polisher at the burgeoning Hudson Scott factory on James Street. Scott's had a work-force of 370 at the start of the decade but with the increase in manufacturing that figure was constantly rising with the number of women and girls being employed before the end of the decade being twice that number.

Jim and Mary Ann had become more than just friends by the end of 1897: their closeness was confirmed when they were married on 23 May 1898, and their closeness was confirmed still further when their first daughter was born on 4 October, later that same year (you do the maths!) Margaret Isabella (Maggie) was named after both of her grandmothers.

During the same week of his wedding, Jim sidestepped the Whitsun Hirings by getting an extension to the contract he secured six months earlier. It would appear there was much call for such work as the wet winter and spring caused havoc in the agricultural industry. The *Carlisle Journal* of 3 June 1898 gives an insight to the working and climatic conditions of the time:

> *We had a taste of May weather for the first time towards the end of the month. The heavy rains which we have experienced have washed in the top dressing applied to grass and corn, and it looks as if farmers who have used artificial this year will be amply repaid for their expense.*
> *The hiring terms has fallen at an inconvenient time this year in these days of dear labour and low prices.*

As the new century dawned, the conditions in which the young Curran family was living had changed little since their parents had set up home thirty years earlier. Eighteen months after their marriage, Jim and Mary Ann secured a tenancy in Hopes Court (again in Caldewgate). This was a small court with desperate, one-up, one-down properties that not only adjoined side-to-side, in terraced style, but also front-to-back; this allowed natural light in, on only one side of the building. Then, as now, the more things changed, the more things stay the same.

So it was locally, and so it was nationally. The country was still governed by men who derived their importance from ownership of land, status and love of Empire. And – as with thirty years earlier – events in South Africa were gripping the nation and attracting international attention. In1870, diamonds had been discovered in the Orange Free State, and the dollars signs in the eyes of Imperialist British politicians could be seen from miles around. This was one episode in Britain's long uncomfortable relationships with the Boer farmers who occupied the South African colonies. Now, at the turn of the century – with gold having been discovered in the Transvaal – Britain was in the middle of a full blown, bloody war with the Boers.

National and local press gorged on the news from the war as the population of Britain became transfixed by events from towns with funny sounding names and were all too eager to cheer on emerging heroes like Winston Churchill and Robert Baden Powell. But as with all wars, flag-waving patriotism and belief in the initially obscure cause soon gave way to unrest and disinterest, as first, news of thousands of casualities, and then, news that Boer women and children were starving to death in British-run concentration camps, left many people feeling disillusioned about officialdom and Empire.

For generations, the masses had simply done as they were told, but now social unrest was leading to their lives being altered, as fundamental change was taking place in their awareness, their expectations and their work. The Currans were a typical example of the urbanised, youthfulness of the country: the census of 1901 recorded that over 25 million people lived in towns, 4.5 million in London; 7.5

A typical court in Caldewgate c1904 (photograph courtesy of Ashley Kendall)

million elsewhere, while 42.5 per cent of the population was between the ages of one and nineteen. A year before the census, Jim and Mary Ann celebrated the birth of their second daughter, Elizabeth Ellen (Lizzie).

Throughout the previous century, class politics had been mantra of successive Conservative and Liberal imperialist politicians for generations. But these changing times – if not carefully monitored – threatened national unity and a weakening of Empire. Out of a population of 45 million, 34 million were working class and it was therefore imperative that an antidote be found to the poison of class antagonism – it was no good conquering the world when the masses back home were threatening to revolt.

The working classes had, therefore, to be brought into the fold and made aware that pride in the Empire gave benefits for all. Empire Day was introduced on 24 May 1902 (Queen Victoria's birthday – the Queen herself had passed away in January 1901). The day was introduced as a feel-good day for all in work-places and schools throughout the country and Britain's dominions. But no amount of feel-good celebrations pays the rent and puts food on the table. Wages were stagnating and, in spite of the relative cheapness of imported foodstuffs, the cost of living was rising. Jim and Mary Ann's problems were exacerbation – albeit self-inflicted – by the further appearances of little Currans as the decade progressed: John James (1902 – named after Jim's father and brother), James (1904 – named after his father and known as Jimmy), and William Thompson (1905 – named after his maternal grandfather and known as Billy), all swelled the numbers in the tiny Caldewgate dwelling. By the time Billy was born, his two older sisters, Maggie and Lizzie were both attending St Bede's school and were benefiting from an education never before seen for the working classes.

The last major education act was passed in 1902 and sponsored by the Conservative Prime Minister James Balfour. The Balfour Act of 1902 abolished the old style school boards and transferred educational responsibilities to the new style all-purpose local authorities. That notwithstanding, for some, priorities – like charity – began at home as one contemporary of the Curran girls admitted in later life:

> *I had to do lots of jobs for my mother. I never went to school on Mondays as it was wash day. I had to look after the little ones and there were lots of errands to do. The school board man from the corporation came knocking on the door in the afternoon and my mother would tell me to run and hide. My mother said she could get into trouble, but it didn't make any difference, as the work had to get done.*

Nationally, the Tories reigned supreme, and the masses were crying out for more than educational reform; the need for social change and representation of the ordinary people became urgent. For four years after the end of the Boer War, bitter conflicts raged over social injustice, and socialism gradually reared its head in an attempt to address the basic concerns of the working population. James Keir Hardie had become the first Independent Labour MP in 1892 – he was re-elected in 1900, the same year the Labour Representation Committee was established. Constant disputes over wages, exploitation of workers and terrible living conditions, culminated in 29 MPs being elected from the re-branded Labour Party at the 1906 General Election, to make it a three party House of Commons for the first time in its history.

But the big winner at the 1906 election was the Liberal Party, achieving a landslide victory over the Tories, and among the scores of Liberal MPs who were returned was Winston Churchill, who had defected from the Conservatives in 1904, after falling out with the party leadership; the Tories would remember this betrayal. But for now, the country had spoken and had decided to renounce imperialism following the disastrous Boer War.

Sir Henry Campbell-Bannerman was the new Prime Minister but it was two of his cabinet that would usurp the limelight and dominate British politics between them for the next fifty years. Churchill was one, while the other was his apparently strange bedfellow, David Lloyd George – the 'Welsh Wizard'. Strange because whereas Churchill's blood was bluer than anyone's, Lloyd George was the darling of the masses, coming as he did from the other end of the social spectrum and class system. He was elected to parliament in 1890, and had shot to fame by his scathing criticism of Britain's involvement in the Boer War. Campbell-Bannerman made him the President of the Board of Trade. Winston had, two years earlier, controversially crossed the House to the Liberal benches, and he too now he found himself in the cabinet.

And change and improvements were gradually realised for the working classes. Although plumbed-in bathtubs remained a strictly middle and upper class luxury, municipal bath-houses meant that for the first time, ordinary families – even those who didn't possess one of the prized tin slipper baths – could now get their bodies clean on a regular basis.

Access to affordable food also became widespread as people had the luxury of choice and improvement to their diet. Cheaply processed marketed foods like margarine, mustard and jam found their way on to working class tables, while prices for staples, such as tea, bacon, flour, bread, lard and sugar, stabilised. And finally, with the import of refrigerated meat, the necessity among the poor to buy 'slink' (prematurely born calves) or 'broxy' (diseased sheep) thankfully receded, although in large households like the Currans, tripe (cow's stomach lining) was still the most popular meat dish.

Jim Curran was not doing too badly by the middle of 1907; keeping a wife and five children was no easy task for a field drainer-cum-labourer-cum-anything else that was going, but he was managing. But any improvements to the national economy and life for the working classes were proving to be at best, fragile, at worst completely unsustainable.

The country again sunk into an economic recession by the end of the year, and unemployment was destined to almost double to 7.2 per cent over the next two years. The well-meaning, reforming Liberals certainly wanted to create employment and fund pension schemes; the question was where was all the money going to come from? An ill Campbell-Bannerman resigned as Prime Minister (he died two weeks later) to be succeeded by the Home Secretary Herbert Asquith. Asquith inherited another prickly question – that of self defence, as the big hitters of European politics continued to increase their military muscle.

By 1908, Lloyd George and Churchill shared the view that there was a clear need for imperial defence in light of the strides made by Britain's major imperial rival: Germany. Unlike Britain, Germany had found the balance of funding self-defence and social justice. Both British cabinet members travelled to Germany – Lloyd George to look at unemployment insurance, and Churchill to marvel at Germany's military capabilities.

In the Curran household meanwhile, on 4 January 1908, five became six when Edward (Eddie) was born. What poor Mary Ann must have thought with another mouth to feed is pure conjecture but such was the existence of working class women during this period. One thing was for sure, extra income would be required for this burgeoning family in these hard times. And an opportunity for Jim to bring in extra cash was just around the corner; it came as a result of reforms made by another skilled operator in the new Liberal cabinet.

Upon taking up office, the Secretary of State for War, Richard Burdon Haldane, found that the army – so unprepared and ill equipped for the Boer War – had change little in the intervening years; it remained a diverse jumble of small units, incapable of effective use, and badly in need of reform.

While Churchill chivvied and lobbied for naval reform, Haldane set out his three-year plan to modify the land forces in preparation for possible continental conflict between the increasingly nervous great powers of Europe. His intention created a genuinely national army, with its regulars available when necessary for immediate deployment, a Special Reserve providing immediate back up, and a Territorial Force furnishing a basis for expansion and support.

In 1907 Haldane's Territorial and Reserve Forces Act received Royal Assent. He summoned the Lords-Lieutenants of each county to a meeting at Buckingham Palace on 26 October 1907, and pressed upon them the duty of energetically co-operating in launching the new County Associations. Jim Curran read with interest as the *Carlisle Journal* reported on the meeting the following day and the consequences for the local part timers:

> *Under the first major army reforms since 1881 (The Cardwell Reforms), the Militia and Volunteer Force both now cease to exist. In their place the Supplementary Reserve and Territorial Force have been created. Under new terms of service, Militiamen are encouraged to join the Supplementary Reserve and Volunteers to join the Territorial Army.*

In terms of its organisation, equipment and training doctrines, the Territorial Force closely followed the models of the regular army. However, the men had no obligation to serve overseas (although this had been said before – prior to South Africa – six years later it was now a similar story). Lord Herbert Kitchener had been Commander in Chief during the South African war. He didn't see anything wrong with the army as it was and he was one of Haldane's strongest critics. He sneered at the new Territorial Force as, "A town clerk's Army."

Major changes had previously affected the local regiments in the Cardwell Army Reforms referred to in the *Journal* piece; the basis of these 1881 reforms was the territorialisation of the infantry. Regiments adjacent to one another but with only one battalion were joined. So in the case of the two local regiments (34th Cumberland, 55th Westmorland), who had been linked in 1873 – with a joint Depot being established at Carlisle Castle – were confirmed as one regiment 1881 with a defined geographical and territorial recruiting area. The Border Regiment was born.

Now, the new 1908 reforms saw the infantry being organised into fourteen Divisions of the Territorial Force. Infantry battalions were aligned to the local county regiments. So, the 1st, 2nd and 3rd volunteer battalions formed the 4th and 5th Territorial Battalions (the 4th Battalion being East Cumberland and Westmorland and 5th being West Cumberland) of The Border Regiment. The local regiment also followed one of Haldane's recommendations and introduced a 3rd Battalion: the Special Reserves; its purpose provided volunteers to act as reinforcement to the regular army battalions and, once mobilised, they would be on the same terms with the potential to be called to serve overseas. This placed the Special Reserves as something between the regular army and the Territorials. Moreover, although all the part timers received the same pay – around 1s per day – the Special Reservists received an additional bounty that saw this figure treble when on duty. Whatever the reservations of Kitchener and his ilk, men flocked to join 'The Terriers,' in this age of and non-work related activity; and one of them was Jim Curran.

Upon entry to The Border Regiment, men were encouraged to learn about the regimental history: its battle honours of Alma and Arroyo; and its service in Asia and Africa. The Territorials did a bit of basic training, weekly drills and attendance at camp; the Special Reserve also attended camps but carried out more training than their TA colleagues. New recruits were drilled constantly, and trained in musketry, Boer War field tactics, military law and organisation, how to recognise bugle calls, and how to work a machine-gun. Jim was joining men from all backgrounds who were happy to give up a night or two a week to train, and the proposed mandatory, annual camp proved attractive to many, as most rarely travelled beyond their hometown or county. One contemporary summed up the initial enthusiasm of the volunteers shortly after joining:

> We had daily cross-country running and the gym exercises and I loved the musketry lessons and the shooting on the firing range with .22 rifles. There was also a school and a teacher in the barracks where one could go in the afternoon and sit at desks with pen and paper to improve one's education. There were examinations, and we could get a third-class certificate. If you were also a first-class shot with the rifle you got sixpence a day on your pay.

Probably attracted by this incentive, and the additional bounty of the Special Reserves, it was this 3rd Battalion of the Border Regiment Jim Curran joined in the autumn of 1908, signing up for an initial six months service at the depot followed by seven years service as a reservist.

3
The Trouble with Alliances

THE need and desire for such military reform was obvious when Britain looked out across the channel to see what her European neighbours were up to at the time. In 1901 the Boer War had been won, but at the cost of the country's reputation. The number of men lost, the amount of money spent, and the length of time taken to subdue a relative handful of South African farmers jolted Britain and amazed the world. Among the many interested spectators to this revelation of Britain's limitations, none perhaps was more interested than the Kaiser and the Great General Staff of the German army, who produced a detailed two-volume study of the conflict. The exact extent to which the Kaiser and his generals were influenced by the spectacle of the British Army's performance in South Africa cannot be determined, but certainly they saw little to discourage their own aggressive ambitions.

Britain had led the field in military power for most of the previous century, but after 1900 she seemed to be losing ground to her stronger, continental rivals; as successive rulers and despots continually sought to augment and develop their land-based empires, there was a disturbing (and very real) possibility that Britain might find itself among the European also-rans.

Lloyd George and Churchill had visited Germany to reference social and military reform, but despite this, Britain's relationship with her rival had been on the wane for some time. Since the last years of Victoria's reign, Britain had watched uncomfortably, as the Germans increased their military efficiency and challenged Britain's naval strength. Before Churchill's reconnoitering expedition, the same question was now being posed in the press and in parliament: 'Was Britain falling behind her rival in the arms race?' No sooner had Hildane taken his Territorial Forces Act through Parliament, later that same year (1908), The First Lord of the Admiralty, Reginald McKenna spoke to allay such Germanophobic fears:

> *I think it is greatly to be deprecated that persons should try to speak the belief in this country that war between Great Britain and Germany is inevitable. It is all nonsense. There is no collision of primary interests –*

big, important interests – between Great Britain and Germany in any
quarter of the globe. There is no feeling of ill-will towards Germany. I
say we honour the strong, patient industrous German people.

This did little to assuage many, and that well-known doom-merchant,
Churchill, in particular, would have none of it. Thirty years later, Winston
would be labelled a 'war monger' for making similar noises about German
expansion and Britain's dithering. In late December 1908, he wrote to Prime
Minister Herbert Asquith with his social and military fears:

I have been revolving many things during these few days of tranquillity
and I feel impelled to state to you the conviction that for a long time past
has been forming in my mind. There is a tremendous policy of Social
Organisation. The need is urgent and the moment ripe. Germany with a
harder climate and far less accumulated wealth has managed to establish
tolerable basic conditions for her people. She is organised not on for war,
but for peace. We are organised for nothing except party politics.

Adding to this inter-governmental tension, Kaiser Wilhelm II himself gave
an interview to the *Daily Telegraph* in October 1908. The 21st century reader
could be forgiven for confusing him with a caricature from a Blackadder
episode:

You English are mad, mad, mad as March hares. What has come over
you that you are so completely given over to suspicions quite unworthy
of a great nation? What more can I do than I have done? I declared with
all the emphasis at my command, in my speech at Guildhall, that my
heart is set upon peace, and that it is one of my dearest wishes to live
on the best of terms with England. Have I ever been false to my word?
Falsehood and prevarication are alien to my nature. My actions ought
to speak for themselves, but you listen not to them but to those who mis-
interpret and distort them. That is a personal insult which I feel and
resent. To be forever misjudged, to have my repeated offers of friendship
weighed and scrutinised with jealous, mistrustful eyes, taxes my
patience severely. I have said time after time that I am a friend of
England, and your press - at least, a considerable section of it - bids the
people of England refuse my proffered hand and insinuates that the
other holds a dagger. How can I convince a nation against its will?

This did little to convince Churchill as he and McKenna continued to trade speeches, documents and evidence of Germany's naval expenditure and comparative military strength, Britain knew she had to stay on friendly terms with France and Russia as she was not strong enough to defend her empire against the likes of Germany.

France had lost much of its global empire when Napoleon was defeated, but in the first half of the nineteenth century, she re-emerged as a major global force, both through its growing economic power and its military forces. France was Britain's major rival for influence in the Mediterranean region and had expanding commercial and cultural influences in the Middle East, and also developed settlements, trade stations, and military posts in West Africa and Central Africa. Now, in the first decade of the twentieth century, the socialist movement was gathering pace, as the citizen demanded his share of Liberty, Equality and Fraternity. Russia meanwhile had expanded continuously following the Napoleonic wars (and would be the largest empire in the world by 1914).

The one big loser in this great expansionist game was the Ottoman Empire. The Ottoman Turks, with their mighty army, once ruled from the Danube in the north to the Persian Gulf in the south, and from the Caspian Sea in the east to Morocco in the west. As the nineteenth century wore on, the Ottoman Empire found that the expensive wars she had fought had virtually bankrupted the empire. As the financial haemorrhaging continued, she was experiencing a steady loss of territories to major European states. Moreover, she was powerless to resist nationalist movements (supported by various European powers) establishing their own independent states.

As the Ottoman Empire declined, and the neighbouring empires jostled for position, the one area that remained highly unstable was that of the clutch of countries and states in south-eastern Europe that were linked by the Balkan Mountains. Historically, the Balkans had felt the influence of many powerful empires: Serbia was most affected by the eastern Greek Byzantine Empire, becoming strongly Orthodox in religion; Croatia and Slovenia were influenced by the powerful Italian city-state of Venice to become largely Roman Catholic; and most of Bosnia was heavily influenced by the Islamic Ottoman Turks. The Balkan states' 50 million inhabitants were therefore divided by religious, ethnic, and linguistic differences and already had a long history of conflict and conquest. As the Ottoman Empire disintegrated in the latter half of the nineteenth century, this bitterness and rivalry was exacerbated.

The final European giant of the day was the Austro-Hungarian Empire, whose influence in south-eastern Europe also increased with the Ottomans' decline. The Habsburg rulers faced serious internal challenges in their multinational empire, hence the imperial system being reorganised as a dual monarchy of Austria and Hungary, with its seat of power in the Austrian capital.

With this constant buying, selling and usurping of lands, these superpowers paradoxically, felt the need to court their rivals and generally keep them sweet, in order to protect their own interests. A series of alliances were developed over the same period as the European Empires were scrambling about and extending their boundaries: 1879 saw Germany and Austria-Hungary make an alliance to protect themselves from Russia; the two then joined with Italy in 1882, to stop Rome siding with Russia; Russia countered in 1894 by forming an alliance with France to project herself from Germany and Austria-Hungary; 1904 saw Britain and France sign their *Entente Cordiale*; and in 1907 Britain made an alliance with Russia, closely followed by the *Triple Entente* between Britain, France and Russia – an alliance made because of Germany's deteriorating relations with both Russia and Britain.

Such machinations and mistrust were summed up in the rather controversial (and, at times, comical) 1908 Olympic Games, held in London. Marred by politics and nationalism, the games were blighted from the start when Irish athletes refused to march under a British flag which in turn prompted pro-Irish contestants from America not to dip their flag to the British royalty during the opening ceremony. Finnish athletes meanwhile were told that they had to march under the Russian flag but instead they chose not to carry any flag at all. Once competition started things got worse: races were cancelled and re-run (in one, only one athlete turned up for the re-run so he won the gold medal!), distances of races were altered, and judging throughout was coloured by international relations between countries.

While the big hitters of European politics – knowing the stakes were high – were jockeying for position in the first decade of the twentieth century, the smaller states had their own agendas. In Serbia, for example: they had thrown the Ottoman Turks out and set themselves up as an independent Slav kingdom. The problem with this was that the tiny state now bordered the fearsome and dangerous (and big) Austro-Hungarian Empire. The Serbs goal was to partially break up the massive empire and achieve unification with Croatia and Bosnia to form one Yugoslavian state. And if diplomacy couldn't achieve this, then more sinister means could.

The Black Hand was a secret Serb nationalist society and their mission spread anti-Austrian propaganda throughout the capital Belgrade, and the rest of Serbia. As the group became more powerful, so their ambition grew: they began sabotage, espionage and political murders abroad, especially in provinces Serbia wished to annex. Such was their impatience with their own officialdom; The Black Hand – a group which now included many government officials, professionals and army officers - performed a coup d'ètat in 1905 when their king was murdered. Serbia was thereafter treated like a rogue state. Bitter relations between Vienna and Belgrade were ratcheted up still further on 6 October 1908, when – while the rest of Europe was arguing about who won the 400 metres in London – Austria annexed Bosnia and Herzegovina directly into the Austro-Hungarian Empire in exchange for a small cash settlement with Turkey. Full inclusion into the empire would give Bosnians full rights and privileges but most of the population still considered themselves Serbian.

It seemed as thought the whole continent was in an absurd juxtaposition: everyone was enhancing territories and augmenting their armouries while working with allies to ensure lasting piece. The World (Universal) Peace Conference, the Nobel Peace Prize and the Haig Peace Conference were all introduced and attended by the very governments who – by their actions back home – were hastening the exact opposite of achieving peace.

Much like today, in 1911 the Germans were not backward in coming forward when it came to taking the initiative. But in those days, their sense of

The 1ˢᵗ Battalion, The Border Regiment in Rangoon on Arroyo Day 1911 (photograph courtesy of Cumbria Military Museums)

enterprise was far more sinister than getting up early to put their towels on the pool side loungers; instead, they were all too willing, all too often, to demonstrate their military might to their watching neighbours. So when Winston Churchill became First Lord of the Admiralty in the autumn of 1911 – conveniently forgetting that he once described the navy as '...all rum, sodomy and the lash,' – he set about playing catch-up by strengthening the resources of the Royal Navy to compete with German development.

At the same time changes were being made to the services nationally, forces closer to home were concentrating on their own celebrations. On 28 October 1911 the Border Regiment marked the one hundredth anniversary of its greatest triumph: the Battle of Arroyo dos Molinos. On the same day in 1811, the regiment (then the 34th Cumberland Regiment) fought in a battle during the Peninsular War against the French. The local regiment won the battle and captured six French drums as trophies of their victory. Every year since, the regiment have celebrated 'Arroyo Day' when the 1st Battalion parade the captured drums.

In 1911 the celebration took place in Rangoon, Burma, where the regiment were stationed. In Carlisle however, Jim Curran and his colleagues in the 3rd Special Reserve Battalion also took part in celebrations at the regiment's home depot. Among the celebrations were the reservists posing for a dramatic photograph in and around the entrance to the castle. Two days later, the *Carlisle Journal* made great play of the celebrations:

CENTENARY CELEBRATION OF ARROYO DAY
Saturday was the centenary of the red letter day in the history of the Border Regiment. The anniversary was celebrated in fitting style by the regiment. The 1st Battalion (successor of the 34th) is at Rangoon, where a series of festivities was to culminate in a torchlight tattoo and fireworks at night.

At the depot in Carlisle, the occasion was also commemorated. All ranks wore laurel wreaths in their caps in honour of the day. The picture and colours in the anti-room and the mess room were decorated with laurel wreaths and in the evening the officers gave a regimental dinner which was remarkable for the fact that for the first time in the history of the regiment all five battalions were represented and entertainment was given to the soldiers' families in the afternoon.

The 2nd Battalion which is stationed at camp also held a celebration in memory of the anniversary.

Jim Curran also had further cause for celebration: having received his first stripe as Lance Corporal a year after joining the army, he was, by 1911 celebrating promotion to corporal within the 3rd Battalion. (Such promotions of officers and Non Commissioned Officers in the Special Reserve were permanent like the regular army, and unlike the temporary officers and NCO of Kitchener's New Army – more on them later). Clearly enjoying his three years' service with the regiment, Jim was now regularly earning around four shillings per week (20p) to supplement his civilian jobbing – by now he was a bricklayer's labourer, working on building sites around the town and earning 22s (£1.10p) per week.

It appeared that his promotion to a Non-Commissioned Officer role was in keeping with the man's personality: a broad shouldered man, his thick black hair and big matching moustache set him out as a confident, imposing character, and family legend has it that he certainly ran his house like the archetypal sergeant major. And that big black moustache was certainly in keeping with his military peers; the faces of soldiers young and old sported hair on the upper

The Depot at Carlisle Castle on the same day (photograph courtesy of Cumbria Military Museums)

lip – in fact King's Regulations actually stated, 'The hair on the head will be kept short. The chin and the lip will be shaved, but not the upper lip.'

Jim and the family were still living in Caldewgate at the time of his promotion but they had moved further towards town, to the slightly larger two up, two down property on Simpson's Court, which was an extension of Studholme's Lane – little more than 500 yards over Caldew Bridge from the castle itself. Would Jim be contemplating professional armed conflict at this time? If he had, the likelihood was that it would not come on the continent – despite the bellicose posturing there – but in the land of his own grandfather's birth.

A few months after the Arroyo celebrations, Jim and the rest of the nation watched as Prime Minister Asquith renewed his party's efforts to establish home rule in Ireland. The Liberals had seen their vast majority eradicated in the general elections of 1910 and were desperate for Irish Nationalist support in the Commons. The proposal of home rule infuriated the Protestants in Ulster however, and their protests were supported by the Conservative opposition. In February 1912, Asquith sent Churchill to Belfast to appeal for calm and moderation. His appeal failed and as the months rolled by, sectarian tensions degenerated into violence, while in London, bitter conflict raged across the dispatch box as the pro-Nationalist Liberals clashed with the pro-Unionist Tories.

By spring 1914 civil war looked almost inevitable. *The Cumberland News* kept its readership up to date in April:

> *The Protestant majority in Northern Ireland have affirmed their wish to remain part of the British Empire. They have formed a volunteer army and are believed to have begun procuring rifles and machine guns. Faced with such a rebellion, the cabinet have proposed that troops from currently concentrated in the Catholic south of the island might be used to guard arsenals, and prevent the Ulstermen from getting more weapons. Warships have been ordered into positions just off Belfast.*

It was also known that nationalists were also forming armed camps, but while most of mainland Britain was looking west at the potential troubles in Ireland, a thousand miles to the east, similar problems were bubbling to the surface. In South Eastern Europe Nationalistic feelings amongst Serbs on both sides of the Serbian/Bosnian border were running high.

During the Easter holidays, the German Kaiser travelled to Vienna to stay with his friend and international alley Archduke Franz Ferdinand, heir to the Austro-Hungarian throne. The Kaiser advised Franz of his simple solution for dealing with such troublesome minorities. "The Slavs are born not to rule but to obey. They should be crushed," he told his host. But Franz Ferdinand had a better idea; he was a gentle man at heart, who adored his wife and children, and he thought reform was the best way of keeping the Austro-Hungarian Empire on its feet and protecting his own future in the process. With this in mind – much like Churchill's mission to Belfast some months earlier – he decided to make a hearts-and-minds visit to Bosnia, the small troublesome outpost of the Empire, to smooth things over with the locals.

4

A Quiet Sunday Morning

AS Jim Curran awoke on the morning of Sunday 28 June 1914, I wonder how much he knew about the Balkan states of Serbia and Bosnia, and their connections with the Austro-Hungarian Empire? The chances are, that he knew little about Archduke Franz Ferdinand, heir to the throne of the Austro-Hungarian Empire, or his visit to the small Bosnian town of Sarajevo that was taking place that same day; and what is certain is that he had never heard of a young man called Gavrilo Princip, and his colleagues from the 'Black Hand Gang'. Why would he? No one else had either – but the events that were about to unravel on that fateful morning in Sarajevo, would bring this bizarre cocktail of characters – with all the complexities of their history, religion, national identity and political machinations – to the world's attention, and set in motion a series of irrevocable events that would result in the First World War. And although he didn't know it, it would also shape Jim Curran's destiny.

Bosnia was populated primarily by three groups: Croats (Roman Catholic), ethnic Serbs (Serb-Orthodox) and Muslims (left from the days of Turkish rule). Although not considered by the Austrians as unfriendly, many Bosnian-Serbs felt a strong nationalistic desire to have their province joined with that of their Serb brothers across the river in Serbia; many in Serbia openly shared that desire. The most demanding extremists in Serbia were, of course, the fanatical terrorist group, the Black Hand, and during the spring of 1914, when they learned that the heir-apparent to the Austrian throne, Franz Ferdinand, was scheduled to visit Sarajevo in June, they saw this as an opportunity to assassinate him. Three young Bosnians were recruited, trained and equipped: Gavrilo Princip, Nedjelko Cabrinovic and Trifko Grabez.

The Black Hand had many [Serb] government and army members, who knew about the plot, the three were, in effect, state sponsored terrorists. But the planned assassination put the Serb Prime Minister Nicola Pasic in a major dilemma: if he did nothing and the plot succeeded, the Black Hand's involvement would almost certainly be uncovered, as would its links with the Serbian authorities, which would, in turn, bring on war with Austria – a war that could potentially crush Serbia. On the other hand, if Pasic warned the Austrians of the plot, his countrymen would see him as a traitor. Pasic decided that he would try to warn the Austrians through careful diplomacy that would not expose the Black Hand. He asked his Ambassador in Vienna to discretely suggest to his hosts that it might be advisable for Franz Ferdinand not to go to Sarajevo. On 5 June, a corridor meeting between two obscure mandarins (which seems more in keeping with something from the cold war over 60 years later) took place. Suggestions were made, hints were dropped, no doubt fingers tapped noses, but significantly, the Austrians didn't get the message and the visit went ahead.

Franz Ferdinand was the first prominent member of the Hapsburg family to make a goodwill visit to Bosnia for over four years. The visit would also roughly coincide with his fourteenth wedding anniversary and his wife Sophie accompanied him on the trip. Although many Bosnians had Serb sympathies, it was not considered a hostile territory and security would not be upper most in the minds of those making the arrangements. As it was, Sarajevo's 120 policemen were due to marshal the crowds on the day, as the Archduke and his wife drove through the streets in their open-topped car.

Elsewhere, the world went about its business, oblivious to the events that were about to unfold in that political tinderbox that was (and still is) the Balkans. Much of Australia woke up to yet another morning of drought conditions – little rain had fallen anywhere on the vast red continent since 1911 and the national economy was suffering dreadfully. The French meanwhile were enjoying happier times: renowned for promoting leisure and sporting

Church Street, Caldewgate c1910 (photograph courtesy of Ashley Kendall)

39

activity since the turn of the century, that morning saw the start of the eleventh running of the Tour de France cycle race. In Washington, the reforming President Woodrow Wilson (whose maternal grandfather was born in Carlisle) was putting the final touches to his Federal Reserve System that was designed to both regulate and stabilise the national banking system in America. Elsewhere in the country, the motion picture industry was developing apace, with Cecil B. de Mille promoting *The Squaw Man*, the first feature-length film made in Hollywood, while his rival Mack Sennett was countering in New York by introducing Charlie Chaplin as the Tramp in the hit comedy *Kid Auto Races at Venice*.

Back across the Atlantic, the Liberal Prime Minister Herbert Asquith was spending a working weekend at number ten (instead of taking advantage of the Prime Minister's weekend retreat at Checkers), wrestling with the ongoing problems of national strikes and the 'Irish problem' that had dogged his government all summer and had seen Ulster Unionist and nationalists each forming armed camps and threatening civil war after an impasse had be reached over home rule. And on that quiet Sunday morning in Carlisle, the streets were bathed in sunshine as Jim Curran and his children walked down Bridge Street from Simpson's Court to St Bede's Church on Silloth Street for the regular Sunday mass at 10.30am. It was not common for women to accompany their husbands to church in those days; besides, Jim's wife Mary Ann was not a Roman Catholic. Moreover – after a period of six years since the birth of her last child – in June 1914, Mary Ann was heavily pregnant expecting her seventh.

A thousand miles away in Sarajevo, Bosnia, it was also sunny and warm as Archduke Franz Ferdinand's motorcade was heading for the city hall and a reception hosted by the mayor. Little did they know that terrorists mingled with tourists in the thick crowds along the route, and as they drove along the main riverside boulevard, one of them threw a bomb directly at Franz Ferdinand. Incredibly, it glanced off the Archduke's arm, bounced off the folded car top and into the street behind them before exploding, injuring a dozen spectators and those in the car behind. The perpetrators fled as the Archduke's car sped towards City Hall and safety. One of the would-be assassins, Gavrilo Princip, made himself scarce and disappeared from the main route of the motorcade and went into a food store on the adjacent Franz Joseph Street. There then followed one of those events that rely on a tiny chance or minor error, the result of which changes or shapes history. The Archduke and his wife decided, after their reception at the city hall, to drive to the hospital to visit victims of the bombing – but no one told his chauffeur. In the confusion as to exactly where they were going, the chauffeur took a wrong turn onto Franz Joseph Street.

At around 10.45am, Gavrilo Princip came out of the food store after buying a sandwich to see his prime target driving towards him. An army official, travelling in the same car as Ferdinand realised the error made by the driver and leaned forward to inform him of the change in plan. The driver put on the brakes five feet away from where Princip was standing. The Serbian terrorist realised instantly that chance had happened in his favour; he pulled out a revolver and fired two shots that both found their target. Princip then turned the gun on himself, but was mobbed by the crowd; he was overpowered and arrested within seconds of the shooting but the damage was done: by 11:30am the Archduke and his beloved wife Sophie were dead.

Back in Carlisle, another ordinary day ended; the Curran family, like everyone else, were oblivious to the tragic events a continent away and their possible consequences. The first Carliseans knew about the assassination was when the city's press reported on the shooting two days' later. Reports ran through the series of events as they had happened and commented on the dreadful crimes that had been committed against various Royal families of Europe over the previous quarter century. The editor of the *Carlisle Journal* wrote prophetically:

> *The murder seems to have no political connection, although it is significant that the murder occurred in the capital of one of the two states Austria annexed without paying any regard to the wishes of the other Great Powers of Europe. When the time comes, the death of Franz Joseph [Ferdinand's father] will let loose or give fresh vitality that are now kept in check by the Emperor's personal influence and authority, and the struggle between Russia and Germany will become keener than ever.*

The perception of many was that the Hapsburgs were one of many chocolate box monarchies ruling on the continent. The press reports made no suggestion the murders would have any effect on Britain and no one could possibly envisage the sequence of events that took place over the next month.

Throughout July, the already fragile, Austro-Serbian relations deteriorated to crisis point. For Vienna, the double murders provided the last straw and she prepared for a get-tough showdown. She issued a series of demands, one of which – acceptance of an inquiry by Austria into Serbia's responsibility for the assassination – would prove significant. The rejection of this one demand – and rejected it inevitably was – would give Austria the excuse it was looking for to invade. This squabble between Austria and Serbia was now hurtling out of control; as Vienna took a hard line against Belgrade, the other powers in Europe started checking their Alliances Handbooks to see whose side they would be on. Knowing Russia would come in on the side of the Serbs, Austria went to Germany to ensure their support in any war. The German militarists just wanted to flex their muscles and hardware – with whom, and against whom, didn't really matter. By not finding out exactly what Vienna had in mind, the Germans made a staggering oversight, as it was common knowledge that nothing in the Balkans ever happened in isolation.

The Serbs *did* appeal to Russia for help and the Germans thought the Russians would stay out of the conflict for fear of internal revolution. With this blind faith, the Germans pushed Austria forward. But when Tsar Nicholas mobilised his vast army on 30 July, the dye was cast. Unlike the local news-paper's prediction of a few short weeks earlier, the two colossal European powers were not to wait for Franz Joseph's passing before clashing in a conti-nental catastrophe; war between Austria and Serbia, would mean war between Austria and Russia; that would mean war between Russia and Germany; and that would mean war between Germany and France. The interlocking alliances forged by the European Empires over the previous thirty years to provide security were now the very alliances that would hurl them over the edge of the precipice into what would be four years of global carnage and bloodshed. Gavrilo Princip's gun not only assassinated Franz Ferdinand, but it was also to be the trigger for these alliances to be enacted. Sure enough, Germany, unde-terred by their misreading of Russia's intentions, declared war on the Tsar's empire to the east on 1 August, and – knowing her ally France would support the Russians – declared war on France to the west, two days later.

In Britain meanwhile – even in late July – as Europe prepared for war, the British remained bystanders. The British public were enjoying a heat wave; the troubles of central Europe seemed far away. It was a beautiful summer and people were very relaxed; what had happened in Sarajevo – the killing of a man they knew nothing about – didn't register with the average British citizen. One average British citizen – Jim Curran – had celebrated the birth of his sev-enth child (the author's grandfather) on 17 July. Two things are known about the name of the new-born Curran: one, his father wanted to call him Cornelius and two, his wife Mary Ann adopted the classic, over-my-dead-body approach to the discussion. She would have none of it and instead appears to have attempted to placate her husband by choosing the middle syllable of the tongue-twisting moniker to simply name the child Neil – although the family would always refer to the boy (and man) thereafter as 'Neily'. At the time of his son's birth – other than this minor family dispute – there appeared to be no clouds on Jim's horizon to spoil his life; or anything on Carlisle's to disturb its small-town tranquillity.

Jim was now within a year of completing his first term of military service but evidence of his willingness to continue beyond 1915 came a few months earlier when he achieved his third stripe and the more comfortable life of the sergeant's mess. And as these international machinations were taking place, he was preparing to don his sergeant's uniform once more, as his 3rd (Special Reserve) Border Regiment Battalion prepared to for their annual camp and training exercise in Caernarfon, Wales, scheduled for early August.

Rather than worrying about issues on the continent meanwhile, the Liberal government had concerns a little closer to home; for most of the summer of 1914, war seemed more likely to break out in Ireland than in Bosnia. (In his diary – later published as part of his memoirs entitled *Memories and Reflections* – Prime Minister Herbert Asquith doesn't even mention the events in Sarajevo towards the end of July 1914. Details of meetings that took place regarding Ireland, including the day before and the day after the assassinations are detailed, but no mention is made of the Hapsburg tragedy, which clearly suggests no significant ramifications were anticipated).

A peace conference was held at Buckingham Palace between 21 and 24 July in an effort to placate both sectarian camps, but this ended with futile results. The *Carlisle Journal* reported on 28 July on 'The Irish Crisis: Grave situation; Gun running; Affray between troops and national volunteers; Four people shot dead.' Further down the same page, under the column labelled 'Incidental notes' was the 'secondary' article on the continental issue: 'War Clouds In The Balkans - They are again threatened with the horrors of war.'

But as the *Carlisle Journal* was going to press on the evening of the 27 July, the Balkan issue was becoming less incidental by the hour. The Secretary of State for War, Sir Edward Grey, made a statement to the Commons:

> It must be obvious to anyone who reflected on the situation that the moment the dispute ceased to be one between Austria/Hungary and Serbia and became one which any great power was involved, it could not but end in a great catastrophe to Europe. No one could say what issues would be raised and the consequences would be incalculable.

As the hours ticked passed, during that final week in July 1914, the whole of Europe became restless: Empires postured and positioned themselves, and successive newspaper editions and radio broadcasts replaced words such as 'possible' with 'probable', and 'likely' with 'inevitable.' Three days after his statement to the Commons, Grey's department announced that the recent military manoeuvres are merely precautionary and in accordance with ordinary routine. The Special Reserve section of the Territorial Army – including Sergeant Jim Curran and the 3rd Battalion of the Border Regiment – were ordered to stand-to.

Although everything pointed towards conflict on the continent, Prime Minister Asquith was determined to avoid splitting his cabinet, despite his conviction that war was inevitable. He wrote to a friend:

> *We are within measurable or imaginable distance of a real Armageddon. Happily there seems to be no reason why we should be more than spectators.*

As the country prepared for its August Bank Holiday weekend, his views were shared by the popular press, 'To hell with Serbia' cried one national newspaper, 'the least worthy member of the European family.' The British were only too happy to sacrifice Serbian interests for the sake of European peace. But Britain's view of Serbia turned out to be incidental, because Belgium – their gateway for trade with the continent – was being threatened by Germany and due to yet another agreement signed in 1839 that saw Britain guarantee Belgium's neutrality, they would be honour bound to take a stand if Belgium was dragged into the conflict. The government therefore reluctantly announced on 2 August that, 'A substantial violation of Belgian neutrality would compel us to take action.' On the same day Germany issued an ultimatum to Belgium demanding right of passage for its armies as they prepared to invade France. Britain stood on the brink and held its breath.

Two days later, the Germans entered Belgium. On the same afternoon, King George V – fully aware of his obligations to Belgium and in the knowledge the security of his vast Empire, with its global trading, would be threatened if it remained in a state of inertia – held a council and issued proclamations calling out the Army Reserve, embodying the Territorial Force, and bidding all naval officers on the Reserves and retired list to hold themselves in readiness for active service. Britain was forced to declare war on Germany.

As German troops marched into Belgium in early August, a steady stream of Belgian nationals, promptly marched out to seek refuge elsewhere, and where better than Britain to take a safe haven – after all it was Britain's allegiance to Belgium that had dragged her into the conflict. Within the next few months, the stream would become a flood.

During the 1930s Winston Churchill would be labelled by some as a 'war-monger.' The seeds of such a reputation were sewn in 1914 when he was the First Lord of the Admiralty in Asquith's Liberal cabinet. Believing his fleet were ready for battle, he couldn't wait for the action to commence. He wrote in his diary:

Everything tends towards catastrophe and collapse. I am interested, geared up and happy. Is it not horrible to be built like that? The preparations have a hideous fascination for me; everything is ready as it has never been before. I feel sure we shall give them a good drubbing.

But upon receiving the news, the general public did not share Churchill's enthusiasm. The mood was perhaps best summed up by one who later fought himself. He was due to take a railway journey but when he and his party turned up at the platform, there was a sign that read, 'All trains had been cancelled owing to the outbreak of hostilities.' 'We were all staggered,' he recalled later, 'hostilities? On a Bank Holiday? Why couldn't they think of some other way to start their silly old business?' This silly old business would end up costing the lives of over fifteen million people.

5
Gallipoli. Where?

HALF a world away, on the streets of Sarajevo, Archduke Franz Ferdinand has been shot down and killed. The assassination sets off the dominos of war: pushed by the warlords in Berlin, Austria declares war on Serbia; Russia, bound by a treaty with the Serbs declares war on Austria; Germany, bound by a treaty with Vienna – and looking to flex its military muscles – declares war on Russia; and France, bound by treaty with Russia declares war on Germany. All hell is about to break loose.

As Prime Minister Herbert Asquith was trying to convince himself that Britain may still avoid being involved in the inevitable conflict on 2 August, Sergeant Jim Curran and the Territorials from the Border Regiment were travelling by train for Wales for their annual camp. They were amongst thousands of Territorial units travelling round the country, as it was normal practice for the part-timers to be employed in this manner at this time. But Curran and his colleagues must surely have known that the journey was a futile one. No sooner had he arrived in Wales, tired and tedious after his long railway journey, he and his men mustered alongside their colleagues from the East Lancashire Regiment to prepare for their return home.

As the *Carlisle Patriot* went to print on the night of 3 August, Britain was still at peace – but only just. It had been in a state of great excitement for days, knowing that war was imminent. The following day, Germany entered Belgium and war was declared, and the *Patriot* carried a story from their Caernarfon correspondent:

> *The Territorial Army units arrived in Caernarfon for their annual camp on Sunday night, but they are now being recalled to stand ready for action on the continent. The Welsh town awoke to 3000 territorials from Cumberland and Lancashire marching with their bands to the station in preparation for their hasty journey home.*

An indication of the insignificance given to this story however – even at this late stage – is noted by the fact that it appears on page five of the newspaper beside an article on the Silloth Bank Holiday Bowling Tournament. But war it was to be; 99 years after her last continental conflict, when Wellington defeated Napoleon at Waterloo, Britain was to send her armies to Europe again, and, unbeknown to everyone, no Bowling Tournaments or Bank Holidays were enjoyed for another four years.

As soon as the mobilisation orders were given, cables were sent to the homes of each reservist; so by the time Jim got home, the inevitable telegram with its ominous red seal was waiting for him. Inside was the official notification of him being called up. Within days, he and his colleagues in the 3rd Battalion were acting as the training and processing unit for the two regular battalions, initially in Carlisle itself, before being ordered to the regiment's new war station at Shoeburyness in Essex.

Reactions to the news of war were mixed, as everyone prioritised. In the Curran household there had been yet another new arrival but Jim was unable to register the birth of his son before being ordered to Shoeburyness. Instead, Mary Ann registered the child herself on 11 August – ensuring that he was given the name of Neil and no other.

It was a dangerous world that Neil had been born into. Not only was his father on the brink of being called away to fight in a global conflict, on a scale never before seen, the social and economic environment for families in Britain was becoming increasingly unstable. His first challenge however was to get through infancy itself.

Nationally, two associations had been formed to combat alarming infant mortality figures – figures that had remained consistently high throughout the late Victorian and Edwardian periods. The National Association for the Prevention of Infant Mortality (1906) and the Association of Maternity and Child Welfare Centres (1911) certainly meant well and were a step in the right direction as far as raising awareness was concerned, but by 1914, little appeared to have changed locally. In his annual report, the Chief Medical Officer for Cumberland, Dr Robert Morison commented on the '...startling infantile mortality figures throughout the county'. He reported that, in 1913, 6298 births had been registered (6217 in urban districts). Of these 685 had died before the age of one (10.88 per cent), with 175 dying within a week of their birth and 271 dying within a month.

Although there is no evidence – either recorded or anecdotal – to support this theory; given that there is a six year gap between Eddie's birth (1908) and that of Neil (1914), and consideration is given to Jim and Mary Ann regularly producing six children between 1898 and 1908, there is a distinct possibility

Sergeant training new recruits in Bitts Park in 1914 (photograph courtesy of Ashley Kendall)

that Mary Ann may have suffered one, or perhaps even two, miscarriages or still births during this six year period

Whatever the conjecture, the truth was that here in 1914, she is faced with caring for seven children of varying ages – including a new-born – should her husband be called away, and it is all too apparent that this would be the case. Her two daughters – Maggie and Lizzie – were now teenagers and would be expected to grow up fast and help raise their younger brothers as financial - not to mention emotional - belts had to be tightened. Food would soon be in short supply and prices would be rising, while wages would inevitably fall.

The same fears and apprehensions were experienced in tens of thousands of homes throughout the country, as six divisions of the British regular army were shipped to France by 19 August. They were quickly followed by Winston Churchill; although he was the First Lord of the Admiralty, and therefore not directly involved with the army, he understood the importance of Flanders and the Western Front to the success of the allies.

Sergeant Jim Curran and the 3rd Battalion (Special Reserve) Border Regiment were being readied for action and prepared to head south to their new training base in Shoeburyness in Essex. The regular soldiers in the 1st Battalion Border Regiment meanwhile were coming to the end of two years spent in Maymyo, upper Burma.

On 4 August news reached them that war had been declared, although it seemed to have made no difference to the routine of the men. (There is no actual mention of the outbreak in the regimental diary.) The frustration of the regular soldier steadily increased over the following month however as hostilities commenced in Europe while he was being held up in a remote outpost of the Empire. Finally, and much to their relief, the 1st Battalion The Border Regiment received orders on 20 September to hold themselves in readiness to return to England. It was another excruciating two months before they left for home on 19 November, by which time the war was well under way.

At the outbreak in August 1914, the German cruiser *Brazardt*, and the new fast battle-cruiser *Gugan*, had been in the Mediterranean. Winston Churchill had been pursuing his big navy policy from the moment he entered the Admiralty and he and his First Sea Lord, Lord Fisher had the navy ready for action. Before the second week of August, sixteen British warships were in pursuit of the German ships. To escape capture, the German vessels raced towards Turkey. Turkey's capital Constantinople (now Istanbul) was a hotbed of imperial intrigue at this time; it was the heart of the disintegrating Ottoman Empire that centred on Turkey and stretched from the Balkans to Baghdad.

Turkey was a neutral state but one with pro-German sympathies; she had a figurehead Sultan, but there was little doubt that the country was ruled by the army general and nationalist, Enver Pasha, and there was even less doubt by this time which side Pasha was on. Once the two German warships were safely in her waters, Pasha promptly closed the Dardanelles (the narrow strait separating the Mediterranean from the Sea of Marmara) to all shipping, and refused to allow British warships to pass through the straits in pursuit of the German warships. In gratitude for their refuge, the Kaiser offered the two ships to the Turkish navy and their commander became a Turkish Admiral. This was in addition to the Chief of Staff of Turkey's army who was German, as was the general in charge of training. The former super-power had long been considered the 'sick man' amongst the great European powers; now under Enver Pasha – although it was increasingly dependant on its ally Germany for military and economic aid – it appeared to be in remission.

Further east from the Dardanelles and across the Sea of Marmara, was the tiny Bosporus straight, which linked it to the Black Sea and separated Europe from Asia. In October 1914, Pasha had ordered his vessels to enter the Black Sea to shell Russian ports and sink every ship in their path.

By the end of October, Turkey was officially allied herself to Germany and on 1 November, Britain formally declared war on the former Ottoman Empire. The Dardanelles and the Bosporus were two of the world's great strategic bottlenecks; with them blocked, supply lines to and from Russia would be lost and the allies feared the Turks – secure in the support of Germany – would threaten the oil-rich Caucasus Mountains, not to mention Britain's imperial communications through the Middle East to India.

Much of the British Government's fears regarding the Near East had been lost under the radar of the national and local press, who were focusing most of their attention on the developing killing fields of the Western Front. Sergeant Curran and his Territorial colleagues at Shoeburyness were certainly expecting to be sent their sooner or later.

Forty miles away from Shoeburyness, in Whitehall, Prime Minister Herbert Asquith had added the controversial Lord Kitchener to his cabinet as Secretary for War and as early as their meeting on 5 November the question of a naval attack on the Dardanelles was first mooted. It was Kitchener who feared that the German lines in France might well be 'a fortress which cannot be taken by assault,' and suggested that there might be merit in looking elsewhere.

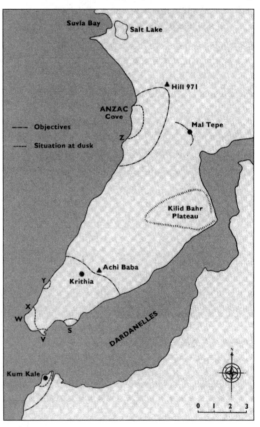

This was music to Churchill's ears. He had already been to France and informed the War Council that the battlefields of France would quickly become bogged down. Churchill's pessimism – entirely justified, as it turned out – about the breakthrough there, encouraged him to push for an altogether different strategy. His navy had already established superiority over the German fleet but paradoxically, this lessened the likelihood of meaningful engagement, as the enemy preferred to hold their fleet in port and

The Gallipoli peninsular with the Dardanelles leading from the Mediterranean to the Sea of Marmara

progress their hitherto successful land offensive. If a breakout from this impasse was to be achieved some bold new strategy had to be devised and Churchill felt he had the answer.

He proposed to attack the German alliance at its weakest point - Turkey. He argued there was merit in forcing a passage through the Dardanelles and inserting his fleet into the Sea of Marmora. By forcing the Dardanelles, the size of the prize – or prizes – were large and plentiful: Constantinople would be taken; Egypt and the Suez Canal would be secured; the oil fields in Persia and Mesopotamia would be safe from German attack; countries like Italy and the remaining Balkan states, who were still surveying the situation from the top of the indecisive fence, would now be encouraged to commit firmly to the side of the Allies; and last but by no means least, Russia would be able to import munitions from the Western Allies and America, and export her huge stores of grain – currently bottled up in the Black Sea ports.

Churchill put forward his argument with characteristic vigour. It was certainly an attractive project and difficult for some members of the war cabinet to resist. But there was not unanimous support for the expedition and a rather half-hearted offensive was ordered: the Royal Navy shelled the forts Turkish forts at the mouth of the Dardanelles in late November, but no follow-up action was taken. The Turks, realising that further attacks would be made, began to strengthen their defences with German help.

Another agenda item at that morning's meeting seems at this distance to be more at home in a Monty Python sketch than in a meeting of the British War Cabinet. There was unanimous consensus that the chief protagonist and arch enemy, Kaiser Wilhelm II, should be removed from the British Navy List of Officers. He had been listed since 1880 and it should be remembered that he was the first grandson of Queen Victoria. However, it was agreed that if it came to light that he was listed as being on our side, it might look a little odd.

Christmas 1914 approached in thousands of households around Britain. The pre-war jingoism everyone had, believing that the war would be over by this point, allowing the country to settle back to its Bank Holidays and Bowling Tournaments, was starting to fade. The war wasn't over; in fact it was only just beginning and tens of thousands of neglected wives and children had to make do as best they could without the head of the household – or much money.

A few hundred families in Carlisle were spared such hardship and unhappiness as members of the Reserve Battalion of the Border Regiment were allowed to return home from Essex for a few days. One of those families was the Currans of Caldewgate. Jim Curran spent a few short days at home with Mary Ann and his children. Seeing little of his latest son Neil, the break from duty must have afforded much relief from the endless drilling and apprehension. But already the financial hardship experienced in so many homes was reflected at No. 14 Simpson's Court.

The Mary Ann Currans of this world did most of their shopping at 'Paddy's Market' (Caldewgate was still considered the Irish quarter of Carlisle) and the Co-operative stores, set up some fifty years earlier in order to give relatively low wage earners the opportunity of buying good value mass-produced goods. As Christmas approached, toy prices rose on average by 25 per cent on the previous year so large households like Jim and Mary Ann's had to make do and mend as best they could. And of course if the consumer was being ever more frugal, the traders throughout the city would inevitably feel the pinch as their businesses suffered. The poultry industry for example, experienced a reduction in trade – turkeys, hitherto imported from Austria and Italy dried up; and the there was little demand for higher priced goods, so milliners and tailors' shops had to adapt their services or close.

There were many others who held a far poorer status than the Currans and the Corporation's annual 'Treats for the Poor' system was strained to its limit; but reports in the press suggested that these treats had been distributed fairly and had been successfully carried out, while various local charities helped out with providing presents for the poor children of the city, The Carlisle Bread and Flour Company Limited cooked home dinners at their bakery in Caldewgate and distributed them to the needy on Christmas Day itself.

And the charity didn't stop there: by December there were eighty Belgian refugees in Carlisle, initially supported by bodies like the Catholic Community Society before the Belgian Relief Committee was set up by the end of the year. The weather in Carlisle over the Christmas period reflected the mood of its citizens – it rained throughout as the muted festivities came and went. Jim said his farewells once again and returned south with his Battalion to their camp at Shoeburyness.

In Whitehall meanwhile, the government – and especially Churchill – were confident that this would be the last Christmas of hardship for Britons. He later wrote of his feelings at this time:

> *The mighty enemy, with all the advantages of preparation and design, had delivered his onslaught and had everywhere been brought to a standstill. It was our turn now. The initiative had passed to Britain – the Great Amphibian... It was for us to say where we would strike and when.*

Churchill's idea of an eastern offensive had initially been side-lined, but in early 1915 the Russians did indeed find themselves threatened by the Turks in the Caucasus and appealed for some relief.

On 13 January 1915, the British War Council's mind was made up. It believed – and was soon joined by France in this belief – that an attack on the Dardanelles would not only restore the supply line to Russia, but perhaps even knock Turkey out of the war and possibly persuade the Balkan states to join the Allies. The Council informed The Admiralty that it should prepare for a naval expedition in February to bombard and take the take the rocky peninsular called Gallipoli. The War Council was not unanimous however in its conviction regarding the campaign. Whereas the normally uncomfortable bedfellow Churchill and Kitchener were for the plan, Lord Fisher, First Sea Lord voiced his reservations about the plan as it stood. He and Churchill had endured a thorny relationship since 1912 when Winston was made First Lord of the Admiralty and Fisher publicly criticised his appointment; now in 1915 the statesman and the sailor found themselves at loggerhead again. Fisher reminded Churchill that it was he (Churchill) who had written in 1911:

> It should be remembered that it is no longer possible to force the Dardanelles, and nobody would expose a modern fleet to such peril.

'Furthermore,' Fisher went on, 'the Dardanelles is futile without soldiers. Someone will have to land at Gallipoli some time or other.'

Kitchener however was nervous about committing troops to the peninsular; he had acquiesced to Churchill's lobbying for the campaign but advocated the navy's attempt to force the Straits on its own. 'The Army should not,' he argued, 'be expected to pull the chestnuts out of the fire for the Navy'. Some of his colleagues on the council poured contempt on the fighting qualities of the defending Turks. Kitchener did not share this view - he was convinced that they would fight hard at Gallipoli in defence of their homeland; and so they proved. Another member of the cabinet, David Lloyd George, wrote prophetically:

> Expeditions which are decided upon and organised with insufficient care, generally end disastrously.

6
The Best Laid Plans

MUCH to-ing and frog-ing took place in the early weeks of 1915, over the scale and type of campaign that would be waged in the Dardanelles, before it was finally acknowledged in mid February – only six days before the naval bombardment was due to commence – that land forces would be required to follow up the assault and make the campaign effective. The naval attack itself began on 19 February 1915 and got off to an ominous start. A combination of three battleship being sunk, three others being damaged, and bad weather forced the offensive to be abandoned almost before it had begun.

Back in London, the previously enthusiastic Lord Kitchener was wrestling with another dilemma: where were the soldiers, who would support the naval bombardment, to be found? Kitchener had a difficult decision to make. He had to weigh up the demands of the Western Front, and factor in the amphibious landings in the Near East. The only available army of any number was a half-trained, ill equipped collection of troops from various countries who had found their way to Egypt. Even the, by now, sceptical Kitchener however, realised that these inexperienced men could not carry the fight themselves. He therefore agreed to release the regular 29th Division – previously intended for the Western Front – for the campaign in the Near East. The French Government also offered a Division and 75,000 men readied for action.

The 1st Battalion, The Border Regiment had returned to England from Burma on 9 January 1915 and was stationed in Rugby. They formed part of the 87th Brigade of the 29th Division. This 'Union Brigade', as it became known, was made up of the 1st Royal Inniskilling Fusiliers the 1st King's Own Scottish Borderers, and the 2nd South Wales Borderers. When King George V took the salute from the whole 29th Division on 12 March 1915, the men knew things were moving on apace.

On the same day, Lord Kitchener was informing his friend and colleague from the Boer War, Sir Ian Hamilton, that he was to command the British and Commonwealth troops in an Anglo-French force to the Dardanelles. 'We are sending a military force, to support the fleet now at the Dardanelles,' he wrote, 'and you are to have command. If the fleet gets through, Constantinople will fall of itself and you will have won not just a battle, but the war.' No pressure there then.

The following day, the men of the 29th Division were given their orders and on 17 March 1st Border embarked on the SS Andonia and sailed for Malta, and then on to Alexandria, Egypt, where they arrived on 30 March. At this time Sergeant Jim Curran was still with his Special Reserve Battalion at their barracks in Shoeburyness in Essex. The Special Reserves were the closest thing to regular soldiers and most of there time was spent drilling and exercising, rather than basic training and induction. There was little doubt they would soon get the nod. They believed however, that if – or rather when – they saw action, then it would surely be on the Western Front. Such belief was reinforced when Jim and his follow platoon sergeants were briefed on the use and effects of poisoned gas; army intelligence had established that the Germans were testing and preparing to instigate gas attacks (this intelligence proved accurate when the Germans dispersed chlorine gas for the first time over Allied lines at Ypres on 22 April 1915).

As their regular colleagues were preparing their assault on the Turkish peninsular, the reserves were given leave to return home in groups throughout the early months of 1915. Sergeant Curran was amongst the last group to benefit from this privilege before his expected deployment. He and his colleagues arrived back in Carlisle in April 1915 to find the city in the grip of the inevitable war-time recession. The cost of living was steadily rising and the *Cumberland News* was keen to highlight the difference in current food prices to those a few short months earlier before the war:

> *A general rise in food prices has seen Carlisle households have to tighten their belts still further in these troubled times. Cumberland bacon is still the normal price but other products are exceptionally high as this chart shows.*

Pre war prices per pound		Today's price
Flour	1*s*/6*d*	2*s*/2*d*
Meat	10*s*	11*s*
Fish	4/10*s*	11/15*s*
Sugar	2½ *d*	4½ *d*
Tea	6*d*	9*d*
Cheese	8*d*	11*d*

With seven children to feed the effect such increases had on the likes of

Mary Ann Curran could not be overstated. She had to supplement what Jim could send home with taking on any menial work that was available. Despite barely being in their mid-teens, Maggie and Lizzie were also expected to find work. The atmosphere in the Curran household at this time can only be guessed at. Jim knew that this would be the last time, for some time, he would be home. He knew about the probability of going to France but before he and his colleagues had left Essex, he had learned about the possibility of being sent to Egypt to support the regulars from 1st Border in their Near East campaign, although the invasion there was not anticipated to cause great problems.

There (Egypt), preparations were being made by the allied army for a landing on the Gallipoli peninsula and on the south side of the Dardanelles. The restrictions placed on available forces by commitments on the Western Front, made the waiting army a strange hotch-potch of invaders. Although the campaign is synonymous with the volunteers of the Australian and New Zealand Army Corps (Anzacs) – and it is perfectly true that the Anzacs distinguished themselves throughout the campaign – there were also representatives from the Royal Naval Division, as well as the British 29th Division, with a battalion of French regulars (and troops from their African colonies) and a few thousand Indian soldiers thrown in for good measure.

General Sir Ian Hamilton had personally witnessed the navy deliver its final bombardment on the narrow straits (which were extremely narrow – eight miles long and in places, less than a mile wide) on 18 March. He decided the best way to take Gallipoli and create the gateway to Constantinople was to launch simultaneous landings on various beaches around the peninsular. While the landings were taking place, two diversions would see the French land on the Asiatic shore, and then withdraw, while the navy would mount a mock assault at the neck of the peninsular – both were designed to confuse and distract the defending Turks.

But hesitancy amongst the British hierarchy crucially led to a five-week delay in following up the naval assault and this proved fatal for the allied forces. Moreover, the maps that Hamilton and his staff were referring to in planning the assault had been drawn over 60 years earlier during the Crimean War.

Ship after ship steamed into Mudros Harbour on the island of Lemnos in the eastern Mediterranean, until there were some two hundred anchored there. The frustration amongst the soldiers of the 29th Division at the interminable delay was eased somewhat when they were informed that the landings would now take place on 25 April. The 75,000-strong army stood ready.

Part of this army of course, consisted of the 1st Battalion The Border Regiment and they embarked at Alexandria with twenty-six officers and 927 other rank. On the 12 April they landed at Lemnos. Among the officers of the local regiment was Captain Geoffrey Morton. The delay in following up the naval assault was not lost on officers like Morton who, upon arriving at Lemnos, wrote home prophetically:

Mudros is a big land-locked harbour, surrounded by bare hills and small Turkish villages of some eighty houses apiece, nestling in the folds of the valleys...The proposed programme of operations is of extraordinary interest... Yet I believe the Navy has made a premature start, and that the Army may have to pay a heavy price in carrying out that which some weeks ago could have been occupied without resistance... Naturally, for every day's delay, the enemy's position is getting stronger and I fancy they know perfectly well what is coming... I will be a memorable night and day when the flag does fall, and it will be but the beginning of many days.

Morton's letter was not published until many days after the landing; in fact coverage of the assault was generally low key. It so happened that the landings had taken place on Jim Curran's 36th birthday and if the part-time soldier had managed to read the newspapers that week, he would have been left in no doubt as to where his destiny lay; two days after the Gallipoli invasion, *The Times* paid little regard in its leading article:

The news that the fierce battle in Flanders on Thursday 22 April is being continued with unabated fury is coupled this morning with the news that the Allied troops have landed at Gallipoli. But the novel interest of that enterprise can not be allowed to distract us from what is, and will remain, the decisive theatre of operations. Our first thoughts must be for the bent but unbroken line of battle in the West.

The truth was that – unbeknown to most people in Britain – the Gallipoli assault had been an unmitigated disaster. In the five weeks between the naval bombardment and the amphibious invasion the Turks had had ample time to prepare adequate fortifications. Amid the chaos of the invasion, allied troops were cut down in their thousands and, despite the Australian and New Zealand troops winning a bridgehead on the Aegean side of the peninsula that would thereafter be named 'Anzac Cove,' none of the main landings had achieved their objectives. At the end of 25 April – the day of the invasion – thousands of men lay dead; thousands more wounded. No regiment could be described as 'lucky' amidst this insanity, but the Border Regiment's losses were considerably less than many others: three officers and 25 men killed, and 78 wounded. 30,000 exhausted men had somehow made it to the shore that day. Hamilton's words of inspiration? 'You have got through the difficult business, now you only have to dig, dig, dig, until you are safe.'

The trouble was, the Turks were dug in too and at this very early stage – despite the likes of Churchill telling himself what he wanted to hear – Kitchener and other members of the Government started to doubt the wisdom of the campaign; an enterprise which was meant to resolve the stalemate of the war, had only produced another front and another expensive stalemate. During the next month of recriminations and I-told-you-so's, Lord Fisher, the First Sea Lord, who did little to hide his grave misgivings about the campaign from the outset, resigned his position, citing his continual inability to agree with Churchill over the Dardanelles as the main reason.

Much of this behind-the-scenes doubt and reproach was initially lost on the British public as, in its blissful ignorance, the press coverage remained upbeat about the campaign. Fortunately for Churchill and others, there were other atrocities to occupy the readership of Britain. None more so than the sinking of the British passenger steamship *Lusitania*, which caused shock-waves on both sides of the Atlantic. The Cunard Line vessel had set off from New York on 1 May, bound for Liverpool with her shipment of meat, medical supplies, copper, cheese, oil and machinery. Shortly after two o'clock on the afternoon of 7 May, she was torpedoed without warning by a German submarine, off the southern coast of Ireland. The giant liner sank in less than twenty minutes with the loss of 1198 lives, including 128 Americans.

The Germans justified their actions by asserting that the ship was carrying arms for the Allies (which later research proved to be true) and that Americans had been warned against taking passage on British vessels in a notice that had appeared in American morning newspapers on the day the ship sailed from New York City. Many in America pressed President Woodrow Wilson to declare war at this point but Wilson chose a diplomatic course, demanding the German foreign ministry disavow the sinking and make reparations. Germany refused to accept responsibility for the tragedy but did agree to sink no more passenger liners without warning. America finally entered the war two years later after British agents intercepted and decoded a message from a German minister to Mexico seeking a German-Mexican alliance against the United States.

Now it seemed as though the enemy was prepared to descend to any bar-barity and the ancient idea that civilians should not be involved in wars was gone forever. Spurred on by the press in London and Washington, hatred of the enemy rose to fever pitch after the atrocity; the knee-jerk reaction for revenge and the desire to kill Germans became a major object in itself.

As an angry and bewildered public tried to come to terms with the heart-wrenching injustice of events like the *Lusitania,* the blame game inevitably started. The jingoism and optimism was fast subsiding and once the true detail of the disaster of the Gallipoli landings started to filter through to Britain. The people learned that many of the British soldiers – their sons, their husbands, their fathers – had been massacred by the well prepared Turkish machine gun-ners; thousands hadn't even got ashore and had been killed at sea. With these horrendously chilling revelations – coupled with the deadlock in France – there developed a growing unease amongst press and public that the Asquith Government was mishandling things, and the war, which was expected initial-ly to be short and victorious, might be long and lost.

The operation in the Dardanelles quickly began to mirror what was happen-ing elsewhere: a campaign that was only supposed to last a few weeks was now looking like a long, bloody struggle with no end in sight. Within a week of the initial landings, the losses were already staggering and reinforcements were in urgent need. Jim Curran finally learned his fate whilst he was still in Carlisle in late April. He returned to his base at Shoeburyness and prepared to sail for Alexandria.

The agonies of pre-war goodbyes have resonated through the generations. Is there any one of us fortunate enough to have avoided such a tortuous expe-rience who hasn't tried to imagine what it would be like? What would we say to a loved one as we left, or watched them leave? Today, the 24 hour news media demand that such scenes are played out in public for the entire world to see. In 1915, the situation was more subdued. The scale of loss in Europe and elsewhere was not lost on the ordinary families who endured their father, hus-band or son leave, after being told he was doing his duty; the home-lives of these millions of people had been altered forever in just a few short months, with no possibility of ever returning to the normality and innocence of their everyday pre-war situations.

Jim left Carlisle in the early days of May 1915. What was said between man and wife would never be known, other than the family anecdote that suggested that the strict Catholic head of the family left instruction for his latest son Neil to be christened at St Bede's Church. What he didn't know (nor probably did

Mary Ann herself at this stage) as he left, was that he was not only leaving his wife to fend for herself and their seven children in incredibly challenging circumstances, he was also leaving her pregnant again. Once at Carlisle station with his colleagues, Jim ceased to be father and husband, and became Sergeant Curran once more. He made the uneventful journey back to Essex and prepared for embarkation on 10 May.

The northern Egyptian port city of Alexandria was the final departure point for all allied troops who were bound for the expedition to the Dardanelles, as it was strategically ideal for the last leg of their journey across the Eastern Mediterranean. Upon arriving there on 21 May, Sergeant Curran and his men faced their first challenge of the campaign: acclimatising to their alien surroundings; although Curran himself was by now an experienced soldier, he and his colleagues had never been abroad before.

What welcomed them in the port was a flotilla of transport and store ships, shuttling men and equipment back and forth, while the docks were awash with troops from all corners of the globe, like the Cumberland and Westmorland men, here to bolster the invading forces on the Turkish peninsular. And it wasn't just the low-born nobodies from the Empire who were doing their bit: they were joined by the likes of Jack Churchill, whose brother Winston had been so instrumental in engineering the campaign in the first place, and the poet turned soldier Rupert Brook whose poems from the period have resonated through the generations. It was Brook who originally conveyed the feeling of optimism and excitement as the original expedition prepared to set out from Alexandria a few short weeks before:

> *It's too wonderful for belief. I had not imagined fate could be so kind. I suddenly realised that the ambition of my life was to go on a military expedition against Constantinople. Oh God, I've never been so happy, I think – like a stream flowing entirely to one end.*

'End' was the operative word: Brook fell sick and died before the expedition sailed. Neither he, nor anyone else could have predicted the staggering numbers that followed him during the forthcoming months. After disembarkation, Curran and the local regiment marched five miles west of the city, to their tented camp at Mex. The heat was blistering and the camp uncomfortable with its amphitheatre of sand dunes being disrupted by the constant winds, creating a dense mist of sand for the men. 'We ate it and drank it' wrote home one of the soldiers dolefully. The already deteriorating morale of the men was compounded still further as they witnessed over-crowded hospital ships arriving with wounded and dying colleagues from the front.

The heat haze distorted Alexandria itself, giving it an even more exotic and mysterious appearance. By day, the locals went about their business in the claustrophobic alleyways and colourful bazaars, while the *muezzin* intermittently droned across the city calling the Muslim population to prayer; by night, its characteristic changed as the streets swarmed with allied troops, who mixed cordially in the cafes and tried to put their worries to one side for a few hours, knowing they would soon be together again in a far more hostile environment. That time was getter ever nearer for Jim Curran.

7
Nowhere is Exempt

MAY, 1915: death and destruction; mangled bodies and machinery; scores of soldiers killed and injured. But this wasn't the Dardanelles – although the same horrors were certainly being played out there – this was much closer to home.

On Saturday 22 May, 470 young recruits from the 7th Battalion, Royal Scots were following Jim Curran's path; eager to burgeon the forces in Gallipoli, they were on a train hurtling south through Scotland to meet the *SS Aquitania* at Liverpool, bound for the Dardanelles. They had sat, frustrated in their barracks in Larbert, Stirlingshire for two days because of a shortage transport, and the news that their troop ship had been stranded in the mud in the Mersey Estuary only compounded their restlessness. Finally, they had been given the green light and their three-week journey had begun when their train had pulled out of Larbert at 3:45 that morning.

Meanwhile, two express trains had left London a few hours earlier, around midnight; the first was bound for Edinburgh and Aberdeen, while the second headed for Glasgow. Six hours later, the latter train found itself sitting in the Kingmoor marshalling yards having a new engine added to it, to assist the express engine as it prepared for the tortuous lug over Beattock summit. Three miles away, the train bound for the Scottish capital pulled into Carlisle station half an hour late. Both northbound trains groaned with holiday makers travelling north for the Whit weekend and lucky soldiers coming back home from the front for some well earned leave. As the Edinburgh express pulled into the station, a similarly delayed heavy goods train pulled out preparing to travel north, heaving its 45 laden wagons behind it.

Morale among the troops travelling south from Scotland was high. Despite the rather depressing stories emanating from the Near East, the soldiers carried the self belief (as we all do) that it would be they who could make the difference; training over, now was the time for action. Men initially dozed and chatted idly but three hours into their journey, most were fast asleep. Also trundling towards the border ahead of the troops was an empty coal train. It had delivered its load to the Grangemouth Naval Base and was returning home to Pontypool in South Wales.

At Gretna meanwhile, two signalmen were about to inadvertently cause the worst railway disaster in Britain's history. James Tinsley and his mate George Meakin had an informal arrangement that saw one or the other start work half an hour later than schedule. On this occasion it was Tinsley – due officially to start at 6am – who benefited from the unofficial practice.

At 6:14am the heavy goods train from Carlisle wheezed its way towards the tiny hamlet of Quintishill, near Gretna, and was shunted into the sidings by the tired Meakin, in preparation for the passenger trains passing; all was silent accept for the birdsong and the goods train that sat patiently, breathing heavily into the beautiful early spring morning. Four minutes earlier, another local passenger train left Carlisle for the relatively short journey to Beattock, picking up the tardy James Tinsley at Gretna on the way. So the players in this historic tragedy were complete: several fast and slow moving trains, ignorant of each other's existence, and two negligent signalmen who could never have believed that their innocent 'Spanish Practice' could have such catastrophic consequences.

At 6:30am James Tinsley arrived at Quintishill and the confusing countdown to disaster started in earnest. Two minutes later, Meakin learned that the troop train was passing through Lockerbie and shunted the southbound coal

Chaotic scenes as bodies are laid out in a field after the Quintishill disaster (photograph courtesy of Ashley Kendall)

The roll call of the Royal Scots after the Quintishill disaster (photograph courtesy of Ashley Kendall)

train into the sidings to let the faster moving train pass. But, disastrously, he changed the points and also shunted the local passenger train onto the southbound line to let the northbound Express train pass on its way to the Scottish capital. Whereas this is not an uncommon practice, it is wholly reliant on one man controlling both north and southbound traffic. After doing this however, Meakin sat down to read his paper and handed over control to Tinsley. Forgetting that his colleague had blocked the southbound line with the very train he himself had hitched on, minutes earlier, Tinsley gave the 'line clear' signal to the troop train.

Finally, at ten minutes to seven, it is time for George Meakin to go home. He turns to leave and sees the troop train hurtle past, with its sleeping soldiers completely unaware that the Carlisle-to-Beattock train is standing idle on the southbound line only yards ahead. Two seconds later, 80 tons of iron slams headlong into the stationary northbound train with such ferocity, that both engines fractured upon impact and are lifted from the track as the following troop-laden carriages scream towards the point of impact, forcing them into the air and skewing them across both lines.

Seconds later, before the magnitude of the disaster can fully be comprehended by the two watching signalmen, and barely before the two mangled trains have come to rest, strewn as they were across the tracks, the almost forgotten Glasgow Express – thundering north, with its double-headed engines – crashes into the tender of the troop train, which lay across the northbound track, with an explosive roar that could be heard miles away.

People from miles around who heard the sickening, crunching sounds, thought the horrors of war had come to them. Flocking to the scene to try and help, what beheld them was a scene of incomprehensible devastation, in total contrast with the beautiful spring morning: twisted, blazing trains contained scores of injured soldiers, letting forth deafening, inhuman shrieks of pain. It is said that burning, mutilated men screamed at their officers to shoot them and put them out of their excruciating death-agony; it is also said that officers obliged and were later praised for their bravery in doing so.

Bodies were systematically recovered and laid out and covered in neighbouring fields before they could be removed. A muster of the Royal Scots took place at 11:30am. Fifty unharmed men answered the calling of the roll – fifty out of five hundred. By the day's end, the catastrophic scene had claimed the lives of 227 people, with a further 246 injured.

The Quintishill tragedy projected Carlisle and Gretna onto the national stage, as the unwanted publicity sent shock waves around the country. People struggled to make sense of it all – if the tragedies being reported from the front weren't bad enough, why did this have to happen? Just as the public were coming to terms with the tragedy of the *Lusitania*, now this. *The Times* summed up the mood of the nation:

> *As our men are suffering in foreign lands, it seems that those of us back home can not be spared such cruelty and injustice.*

Two days after the disaster, unreported, two thousand miles away, Sergeant James Curran slipped out of Alexandria for the 700 mile journey north aboard the troop carrier *Orsyra*. He was one of 300 other ranks in a battalion lead by ten officers. The local men – oblivious to the tragedy back home – were heading for their own disaster zone; but in this idyllic calm before the storm, they enjoyed a beautiful Greek sun, as the ship picked her way towards Lemnos, through the scores of islands, with their picture book tiny villages of white limestone houses with their red roofs that dotted the hillsides. The incongruity of this Mediterranean idle with their ultimate mission must surely not have been lost on Jim and his colleagues. Ancient Greek mythology had it that Jason and his Argonauts rested at Lemnos during their journey to the world's end to find the golden fleece; now the traveller from Caldewgate and his men from Cumberland and Westmorland were resting prior to the culmination of their own odyssey – whether it would be successful or not remained to be seen.

On the 26th they set foot on Cape Helles, at the southern tip of Gallipoli for the first time. Approaching, it was obvious how their colleagues had struggled a month earlier, with the high bluffs acting as the perfect defensive position, while the open beaches below offered no cover from the Turks murderous onslaught. The high ground virtually formed a spine that ran the length of the whole peninsula.

Sergeant Curran supervised the disembarkation of his platoon on W Beach or 'Lancashire Landing' as it was called (this was due to the heroism of the Lancashire Fusiliers on 25 April, who sustained enormous casualties and won six Victoria Crosses that day), before immediately being ordered up to the base of Gully Ravine on the western side of the peninsular, to the headquarters of what was left of the regiment. The ravine itself was situated beyond the bluffs of Gully Beach and ran in a north easterly direction to the foothills of Achi Baba, an area of high ground (and high strategic importance) which was supposed to be the ultimate objective of the Allies, the day after landing. There were a number of shallow ravines the run off the main canyon that was 300-foot deep in places. Allied attacks on the ridges to the west and east of the ravine had resulted in a trench system that led to the front line; these support or reserve trenches however, were also the setting for constant direct and bitter fighting.

From now on, Curran and his colleagues from the Special Reserve Battalion were part of the 1st Battalion The Border Regiment. They were second draft of reinforcements, sent out to bolster the decimated army. Its strength should have been 1,000, split between four Companies (A-D), which

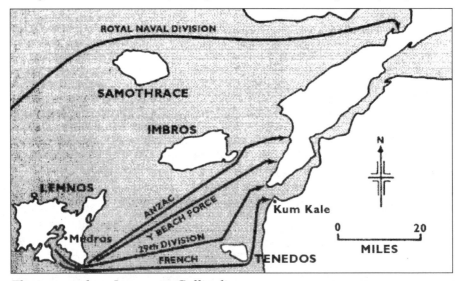

The journey from Lemnos to Gallipoli

were in turn were split into four Platoons ('A' Company Pl 1-4, 'B' Pl 5-8 etc). One regular officer – returning to the peninsular after having been wounded in the original landings – wrote in a letter dated 26 May, the day the reinforcements joined:

> *My platoon, No. 16 D Coy 1st Border Regiment, is a fair average specimen of the landing party, and out of nearly 60 there are only fifteen left...*

Upon arrival, Sergeant Curran was allocated 2 Platoon in 'A' Company. Within hours of landing, he and his men would have been in no doubt as to the enormity of the challenges that faced them. Marching to join their colleagues in temperatures in excess of 30 degrees, they are instantly covered from head to foot in the fine, dry, choking sand that 'penetrates ears, nose and throat', while the two-mile advance is constantly disrupted by enemy shelling. Once at the makeshift Battalion Headquarters, the men look to their platoon sergeants like Jim Curran for leadership and inspiration amongst the dire conditions. What behold them are squalid rat-infested conditions in which their colleagues – and now they – are living. A constant stream of stretcher-bearers scuttle back and forward with the groaning wounded, to any tiny bolt hold that can be used as a dressing station; sometimes a stretcher will pass in less hast with its passenger covered up.

The men were immediately given a rest period where they were given a meal and an opportunity to write home. No doubt there were a few 'arrived safelys' and a couple of 'don't worrys'; but one soldier couldn't contain his revulsion of the camp as he wrote, 'It looked like a midden and smelt like an open cemetery.'

The medical facilities were completely overwhelmed by the casualties. Trench warfare in searing hot conditions, along with the fear of dysentery and other disease rendered the hospital stations completely inadequate. Sergeant Curran and the reinforcements had witnessed the hospital ships coming into Alexandria a few days earlier – they were now seeing for themselves the need for such an expedient. The figures were staggering: in one month 20,000 men had been lost – killed or wounded.

Corpses lay in No Man's Land for days; blackened through the heat of the sun, they swelled and stank. The day before the reservists arrived, the one and only truce of the whole campaign was called to allow both sides to recover their dead, in order to give them a decent burial, (not to mention need to reduce the likelihood of disease, or the physiological effect of seeing a friend's decomposing body a few yards away).

Over-worked Border Regiment stretcher bearers at Gully Ravine (photograph courtesy of Cumbria Military Museums)

Back in Britain, the country was in uproar: every day, wives and families dreaded the arrival of an official looking envelopes that would bring the most feared news possible. What had started off as telegrams to a few unfortunates in the early months of the war had now turned into buff coloured envelopes delivered with the morning post. Somehow, word got around and people started to learn by heart the numbers on the envelopes that were the harbingers of differing news: army form B.104-80 and later 81 dealt with wounds; B104-83 dealt with those who were missing. However most feared was the envelope with army form B104.82B. This document issued by the War Office began without prevarication: '*It is my painful duty to inform you that a report has been received from the War Office notifying the death of: ....*' Such envelopes were now being received by tens of thousands of families on a weekly basis.

In Westminster, the pressure was mounting on Liberal Prime Minister Asquith to form a coalition government with the Conservatives. Asquith opposed the idea of inviting the Tories into the cabinet as long as he could; it wasn't so much the policies as the political style and manners of the opposition he so disliked. But his chancellor Lloyd George realised that this was the correct course and advised his prime minister to heed the call; he also proposed limiting the war cabinet to a smaller, more efficient membership that should not include Asquith, who could then be released to focus his attentions

68

in other areas.

Finally, in late May, Asquith acquiesced and invited the Conservatives to join the government. The Tory leadership were naturally willing pool their skills and resources, but their cooperation would come at a price: they wanted Churchill – the man who had betrayed them in 1904 and who had taken so much pleasure in savaging them through the campaign of the People's Budget – ousted from office. Increasingly marginalised from his Liberal colleagues, Asquith agreed and relieved Churchill from his role at the Admiralty, although he was given a role in the re-vamped War Council, now re-named the Dardanelles Committee.

The first job of the new Dardanelles Committee was to establish the current position and decide on the next phase of operations. The current position was quite clear: with every futile offensive mounted, hundreds of men were being lost as the well dug-in Turks simply held their key strategic positions by showering the oncoming Allies with shot and shell.

The new arrivals had to adjust quickly to this living hell. The enemy and their fortified – almost impenetrable – positions was one thing, the foul living conditions were another, but there was another unbearable opponent that would outdo even these agonies: the flies. Up until the end of May the weather had been reasonable cool and the troops were relatively healthy. Bizarrely, among the mayhem, it had been an idyllic month for foliage, with wild flowers blooming everywhere, even between the front lines. But by the month's end however, temperatures soared and with the heat came the infestation.

Any veteran of the campaign would tell you that the flies were often more horrible that the war itself. They began to multiply in May as the temperature rose; by the time Sergeant Curran and the reinforcements arrived at the end of the month, they were a plague, feeding off the unburied corpses in No Man's Land; on the latrines; and on the food of the men. No one was exempt from the pestilence; no tin of food could be opened without being covered instantly with a thick layer of black, writhing insects. One soldier wrote of the horror:

> *The plague of flies is worse than one can imagine, they are present in millions. A tin of tea will soon contain dozens of them struggling in the liquid whilst there is no part of the bare human body that they will not attack. One eats them with the food and swallows them with the water. We wash and shave with them about our face, hands and eyes. They settle on the dead in clouds, and aggravate the bleeding wounds of the suffering invariably adding to their agony.*

Jim Curran was a toughened veteran, a platoon sergeant who had suffered hardship in and out of the army, but even to such a hardened soldier, it was horribly apparent that these pests – bloated on the feeding of dead animals and men – would have a significant physiological effect on the morale of the men he was trying to lead and inspire. There was no escape for anybody, even when night fell. Mosquito nets were a rarity (and then only for senior officers); one of the most valuable possessions the ordinary rank and file could possess was a small piece of muslin which he could wear over his face as he ate or slept.

Many of the soldiers now believed that they had been overlooked and abandoned by the politicians; the original objectives forgotten. The contrary was actually true – the campaign had finally succeeded in grabbing the attention of national and local press, such was its significance and cost, and they weren't about to let anyone off the hook.

The Carlisle papers had their regular 'News from the Dardanelles' column, which was usually followed by the ever growing 'Casualty List' that named every man killed and wounded. In its piece in early June, the *Cumberland News* reported on the first meeting of the newly formed Dardanelles Committee. But if Mary Ann Curran was hoping to read about better facilities and equipment for her husband she was disappointed. Instead Winston Churchill – determined that the campaign he championed should succeed, despite his being ousted from office and apparently carry the can for its initial failure – lobbied for more troops to be sent to the region. He wrote to his cabinet colleagues arguing that ploughing more men and ammunition into France was making little difference there, but by burgeoning Hamilton's forces in Gallipoli, significant progress would be made:

> *It seems most urgent to try and obtain a decision here, and wind up the enterprise in a satisfactory manner as soon as possible. If the army advanced just three or four miles up the peninsular, the fleet can stream through the Sea of Mamara and all the old objects would still be realised: the collapse of the Ottoman Empire, the support of Russia, the allegiance of the Balkans.*

Where else in the other theatres of war could they look during the next three months for a victory? The Dardanelles Committee met on 7 June and Churchill and Kitchener (by now fully behind the campaign) had little difficulty persuading those present. Three of the largest ocean liners: the *Olympic*, the *Mauritannia*, and the *Aquatania* would be commandeered to take another three divisions to the eastern Mediterranean to unlock the stalemate. Before the month was out, Hamilton would have 120,000 men. The Gallipoli campaign was no longer a distraction to the main events in France; it was the front on which the British hopes were fixed.

8
The F Word

IF you were a newly arrived soldier in Sergeant Curran's platoon (or any other for that matter) at the Border Regiment camp at Gully Ravine, your day quickly fell into a fairly repetitive, if gruelling, routine. It started with the gruff Non Commissioned Officer unceremoniously giving you your early morning call – stand-to at 4am after a restive 'night'.

Immediately you are aware of the rising temperature outside and the flies in your billet; fortunately, they don't bother you so much at this stage, as 'food' is being prepared elsewhere – and of course, there are always the latrines and dead bodies to occupy them. As you rise, and attend to your personal hygiene, they become increasingly interested in you. Trying to wash, shave, clean teeth all becomes a contest; a battle of wills that immediately dents your morale. Your sergeant then leads you forward to your section of trench. There are a series of support and reserve trenches as well as the front line trench; all are narrow and movement is difficult as you and your colleagues frequently meet parties of other regiments on their way out and the effort to pass on another in the cramped space leads to delay and confusion. Once in position, the Turks immediately get your attention with the first shots around dawn.

After two hours you may be given a break from duty by colleagues - this allows you time to return to one of the fall back positions where you may be able to get some breakfast. Breakfast consists of fried, fatty bacon and hard biscuits, washed down with milkless tea. If washing is a contest, then breakfast is an unwinnable farce, as scores of the little bastards cover your food and drink; the only reason it is scores and not hundreds is that 120,000 of your colleagues are enduring the same torture.

After your break, it's back to the trenches to take your place on the fire step – you can't go wrong, just follow the booming sound of the guns. By 7am and the Turkish battery is in full swing, bombarding the trenches with nerve-racking ferocity. During your first couple of hours on the peninsular, you wondered what the strange whirring sound was; now you know instinctively to crouch as low as possible, realising it as the pre-curser for the series of lightweight shells that hail down in and around the trench, sending up clouds of sandy earth and polluting the air with vile smelling fumes. The dust covers everything and everyone: billowing, choking and vile, and the Turkish shells just keep screaming through it. This noise is constant, like an express train in your ear, and all the while you endure the physiological torment of wondering where the next shell will land.

It is barely mid-morning, the noise is deafening and you are covered – head to foot, ears, nose and mouth – in dust. Our own artillery start bombardment the enemy trenches, only yards ahead. You know what's coming next: the platoon sergeant orders a charge. We all pile out of the trench to try and exploit the few yards of ground. It never works – we are driven back in, thankful to be in one piece. The Turks then counter-attack with the same tactic; it never works either – we manage to drive them back and consolidate the line. You lived through this living hell yesterday, you know if you can get through today, you be living it tomorrow too.

By the middle of the day your ears are splitting. If you're lucky your platoon sergeant orders you back to one of the support trenches where you can get a breather and something to eat. Today's menu? Bully beef – always bloody, fatty bully beef, milkless tea and plumb and apple jam: the flies favourite. Then it's back to the front for another four hours of hell and damnation. One of the minor luxuries comes with the evening bath and the days end ritual of brewing some tea and sharing a long conversation under the starlight with your mate – if you've got the energy, and if he's still around. The day ends with the muffled sound of the mule trains, bringing stores up to the front from the beaches as darkness falls.

Finally you retire to the dug-out to try and get some sleep, knowing that quality rest is virtually impossible – the flies will see to that. You burn them off the walls and the ceilings with lighted candles to give yourself some respite but you know they'll be back in the morning. Mentally and physically exhausted, you hope you're not too tired to sleep.

It is staggering how much pain and hardship human beings can endure, when forced. It is said that gradually, the soldiers on Gallipoli, faced with such a continuously inhumane environment, almost removed themselves to another plain of existence. The future virtually didn't exist, as the men – almost droid-like – increasingly lived for the moment; as for the past, it just blurred into obscurity.

Many of their colleagues in France (although in their own hell) had the opportunity of meeting women and children when behind the lines. Such tiny occurrences must have given the troops there some awareness or normality away from the trenches. The men at Gallipoli had no human contact other than with each other, in their brutal environment; the incessant noise, the ever-present dust, the excruciating pain and the physiological torture of the flies all became a natural condition of life.

A few hundred yards west of the camp was the sea. The slopes there had been identified as rest areas for the men, but were in fact more dangerous than the front itself, since – on the odd occasion that the dust cleared and the Turks could to see what they were firing at – the men were exposed in the open areas as obvious targets. But such was the insanity at the front, soldiers persistently took their chance; bathing in the cool sea became an indescribable delight, to escape the flies and wash the dust from the hair and eyes became a wonderful experience.

Into the early days of June and, if it were possible, conditions get worse. Bombarding starts in earnest through the night as well. As darkness falls, rifle fire starts; this inevitably leads to shell fire. Sergeant Syd Evans was a colleague of Jim Curran's in the 3rd (Reserve) Battalion before the war. Following Curran to Gallipoli in early June, Evans described in a letter home the nocturnal nightmare:

> *Shortly after midnight, our guns from behind us join in, and the din became terrific. The continuous crashing of the artillery, the momentary glare of the flashes, the pale ghostly illumination of the lights, added to the heavy rifle fire, and the staccato rat-tat of the machine-guns, combine to create a vivid impression of hell let loose. In addition, batteries of our guns just above the Gully were engaged in blazing away at the enemy to the accompaniment of a series of ear-splitting crashes so that although we were tired out from want of sleep, sleep was out of the question. We did not know until morning that it preceded an attack by our front line of the Turkish trenches. The Turks had recaptured a portion of the trenches and a determined counter-attack was successful, but costly, with a number of our men being killed, including Captain Moore, who had led the counter attack. By sunrise, only a few desultory shots are exchanged and we are able to have a rough breakfast.*

Evans' arrival and that of his colleagues swelled the Battalion to 700-strong, although there were barely 300 from the original landing in late April. As June went on, it was the job of Curran, Evans and the other platoon sergeants to lead their men gradually up the valley to challenge the Turkish positions. Hard fighting took place between 10th and 15th June, with the Border lads having some success in taking one of the defenders' trenches. As Curran and Evans drove their men on, the routine of fighting for a few yards up the steep path of the ravine and then digging to consolidate their advance continued, unabated; all the time, under the murderous fire of the Turks.

One of Evans' men, Private Albert Hunt made a graphic before and after note in his diary:

> *In some parts our trenches and the Turks are only 20 to 30 yards apart. Heavy shelling all morning. We suffered heavily. Hundreds of bombs are thrown every hour, they cause much damage. The Turks are adept at throwing them...*
>
> *...We march into another trench, dead Turks everywhere, feet poking through the ground. Heads and arms showing through the parapets, in places the ground moves under your feet owing to the swelling of the dead bodies buried just underneath, the smell is poisonous. About 500 dead Turks were brought through, some had been lying about for months, we buried them in a spare trench. Enemy made attack but were driven off, on watch all night.*

Gully Ravine, a hive of activity in June 1915 (photograph courtesy of Cumbria Military Museums)

Finally, after being at the vanguard of the assault for seven days and nights, the Battalion found some respite when they received orders to return to Gully Beach for two days' rest. This is 'rest' in the loosest sense of course: the men reverted from soldiers to labourers and sappers as they worked in fatigue parties of 200, day and night, unloading stores, building roads and terracing the side of the cliff to improve accommodation. But still, it made a change for fighting for your life a hundred yards up the ravine.

In the two weeks they had been fighting at the front, the colours of the landscape behind them had changed. Any grass that lay there in the spring had now vanished and – totally incongruous with the barbarism yards away – there were now wide areas covered with beautifully coloured purple flowers of wild thyme, and green figs and pomegranate, with its little flame coloured blossom on the fruit. The paths and roads of course were still something out of the desert with the constant back-and-forth traffic kicking up the ankle-deep dust.

Back at their headquarters, the other major change the men noticed was the increased number of insects and animals that had emerged to keep the flies company in the rising summer heat. Soldiers – many of them new recruits who had never been out of Cumberland and Westmorland before – encountered tarantulas, centipedes, scorpion and lizard in their few square yards of ground. By mid-day the cicadas had cleared their throats and tried their best to outdo the distant shellfire, while the incessant sun burned down mercilessly, turning every trench and dug-out into an oven from four in the morning until eight at night, and making mettle plates and mugs too hot to touch.

Two things that hadn't changed of course were the flies and the poor diet - both combined to spread disease amongst the troops. The NAFFI stores of later campaigns did not exist in Gallipoli and there was no means by which soldiers could access green vegetables. The only minor luxury was a rum ration but this was only doled out at long intervals. The ever resourceful men resorted to throwing hand grenades into the sea to catch fresh fish! But from June onwards, the sun beat down on the trenches where there was no breeze and dysentery and diarrhoea gradually took hold and spread like wild fire throughout the army. The typical gallows humour of the British Army saw the men christen the condition the 'Gallipoli Trots' or the 'Gallipoli Gallops'.

But many weren't laughing as they became so weak they could barely drag themselves to the latrines, let alone fight. By the end of the month, over a thousand men were being evacuated each week. This only led to more farce – medical services were breaking down under the strain. The original intention of setting up mobile hospitals on the peninsula soon after the original landing never materialised – another failed objective. Instead, arrangements were made to establish a base under canvas on the island of Lemnos but this small facility soon became overwhelmed by the increasing number of casualties. The choice for the wounded or ill soldier was one of two: either suffer the rickety journey of a horse drawn ambulance and be dumped on the beach under the baking sun; or, take your chance on a hospital ship that ferries you across the Lemnos, where the patients lay out on the ground in their cord breeches; same conditions, just different scenery. At the front someone invented a phrase that expressed the soldiers' view of the islands: it was Imbros, Mudros and Chaos.

Back at the Battalion Headquarter, the men of the Border Regiment did receive some good news when, two days after their return to base, on 22 June, letters and parcels arrived from home. Parcels contained treats: chocolate, biscuits and dried fruit were an unheard of luxury for the Border lads; and letters contained news, fears and love. For one, a single piece of information covered all three: Mary Ann informed her husband Jim Curran that she was expecting their eighth child in January 1916.

Jim sat in his fox hole – on that dusty peninsular, two thousand miles from home – alone with his thoughts. How would any of us react to such news in his circumstances? Normally filled with excitement and pride but in his perilous position – regardless of the tough character of the man – there must surely be concerns about his wife and her health, the children, and the very real danger that he may never see the baby.

With less than 24 hours to contemplate the news, Sergeant Curran and his men received orders that an attack was imminent in an effort to take the whole of Gully Ravine. The men of the Border Regiment prepared themselves as best they could. The morale boosting news from home soon wore off as the men were issued with ammunition for the big push; afforded a few days of contemplation, they were informed the attack was to take place on 28 June. Some were also supplied with pith helmets, but most wore the same uniform that had been issued to the army in France: the flat peaked cap, the thick khaki serge tunic and breeches, puttees (cloth leggings) and boots. There were no steel helmets.

The objective of the battle was for the combined British, Indian and French forces to attack and secure various key ridges and trenches up the ravine in order to eventually secure the whole of the canyon, which would then give the Allies a significant foothold inland to launch an assault of the strategically vital Achi Baba heights.

The Border Regiment's orders were to take two key Turkish strongholds – the colloquially named Boomerang and Turkey Trenches. The local men were now commanded by Captain Nelson who had himself been wounded at the initial landings, been transported to hospital in Alexandria, and was now back with his regiment only to find he was the senior officer in the field. Nelson briefed his Company Commanders two days before the battle and – knowing that once the fighting started, it would be difficult to harness the men – it was confirmed the commanders would be able to give their own orders. Battalion Headquarters was set up on the west side of Gully Ravine, where Nelson and his staff could monitor the progress of the assault.

On the eve of the battle Captain James Forbes-Robertson who was commanding 'A' Company, called Sergeant Curran and his fellow platoon sergeants together to brief them on the follow day's plan. Forbes-Robertson was a soldier with over ten years experience (he would go on to win a VC in 1918) and had no trouble commanding the respect of his subordinates who understood their commanding officers were in as much peril as they were. Curran and his colleagues knew exactly what was expected of them: orders included being prepared to assume command in case of casualties. 'A' Company was ordered to capture 'Turkey Trench', with support from 'C' Company. ('B' Company was ordered to capture 'Boomerang'). Men who lose touch must join up with the nearest company or regiment and push on. Curran, in turn passed the orders on to the men of his platoon.

The 1st Battalion The Border Regiment left Gully Beach on the afternoon of the 27th and moved up the east side of the Gully to within sight of the two trenches they were planning to take. Sergeant Evans describes the advance – his words are both filled with foreboding and are extremely moving:

> *At 4:30pm we dress in full marching orders and set off up the Gully. The day is intensely hot, the hottest we have had so far, and before we have gone far the perspiration is running off like water. The heat and dust, together with the heavy weight of our equipment is trying and we are glad to halt half way up. During the halt our chaplain conducts a brief service, which brings home keenly all the possibilities that the morrow holds and no church congregation could have been more reverent in its manner. At the conclusion, the congregation broke into that fine old hymn 'Abide with Me'. One felt that never before had any of us sung it with such real earnestness.*

Allied French, Indian, and other British troops all halted their advance and fell silent across the ravine to listen, as the sound of the Border men singing this most poignant of hymns on the eve of battle – possibly their final battle; possibly their final hours – resonated across the scrubland. One soldier from the Royal Inniskilling Fusiliers later wrote:

> *...All of a sudden we heard that old favourite hymn 'Abide with Me' start to drift across the ravine. I found out later it was the Border lads and I'm not ashamed to admit that it brought a tear to my eye as it did with many others in my party.*

What must the defending Turks have made of it all?

9
The Border Lads

THE Battle of Gully Ravine began at 10:45am on 28 June 1915. It was preceded by the artillery letting loose on the defenders' positions – including Boomerang and Turkey – at first light. At 10:30am Sergeant Curran was going round his men making sure that their equipment is in order and everyone was ready. Fifteen minutes later, the shelling ceased. It was time.

Captain John Hodgson from Keswick led the Company's assaulting party; immediately after leaving their positions they came under torrential fire from the Turks. All sixty men were either killed or wounded in minutes; Hodgson was bayoneted and killed, a mere eighteen days after arriving in the Dardanelles. Sergeant Curran was in the follow-up assault that initially fared little better, suffering heavy rifle fire and shrapnel once in open ground. His No. 2 Platoon however – and that of 4 Platoon – made sufficient advances to get across the enemy line and pour into 'Turkey Trench' opening fire on and inflicting significant losses on the defending Turks and forcing over a hundred others to surrender. Sergeant Evans and his colleagues in 'B' Company meanwhile were having success in their assault on 'Boomerang Trench.' But his diary described the horror of such a victory:

> *There are dead lying about in all sorts of grotesque attitudes, British and Turkish alike. Several of our own men are lying dangling on the barbed wire which had held them up whilst they were shot at point blank range by the defenders. Nearby, one Turk is lying with half his head literally sliced away from the chin to crown and presenting a horrifying spectacle, so we hastily throw an old sack over his face. A little further along the trench are gathered some of our wounded being collected, before being sent back to the dressing stations. One has his hand blown off and is groaning with pain. Another young Scot is lying on the ground whilst the less wounded comrade binds up the severe wounds in his chest. A glance, however, shows that he is beyond human aid for his soul is fast slipping from him. In his half delirious way he is moaning something about 'my poor Maggie', I can scarcely keep a lump from my throat.*

In all, the allied attack proved to be one of the few successful assaults of the whole campaign; but like all the others it came at a considerable price: The Border Regiment lost two officers killed, 153 NCOs and men killed or wounded; which represented ten per cent of the whole allied losses. 1st Border, having achieved their objectives then dug in and fortified their position with rocks and boulders – their position became known as 'Border Barricade'.

Barricade was an appropriate word as the Turks characteristically then mounted a series of counter-attacks from positions further up the ravine. Vicious and bloody fighting continued for the following days until finally on 5 July, the Turks mounted their strongest – and final – counter to try and recover their lost ground. They failed and the allies won the battle. Three Distinguished Conduct Medals were awarded to NCOs and men of the Border Regiment. General Ian Hamilton noted the Regiment's efforts. In his colourful dispatch Hamilton appears to make a reference to the Regimental Quick March is *D'ye Ken John Peel:*

> *At 10:45, a small Turkish advanced work in the in the Saghir Dere, known as Boomerang Redoubt, was assaulted. This little fort, which was very strongly sited and protected by extra strong wire entanglements, has long been a source of trouble. After special bombardment by trench mortars, and while a bombardment of surrounding trenches was at its height, part of the Border Regiment, at the exact moment prescribed, leapt from their trenches as one man, like a pack of hounds, and pouring out of cover raced across and took the work most brilliantly.*

Although the Battle of Gully Ravine was considered a victory, it was hollow and futile. The struggles at Cape Helles (the southern point of the peninsular) between April and July simply followed the strict pattern of trench warfare at its most brutal: initial bombardment, followed by the infantry charge, followed by a counter-attack. Net result: status quo.

Nowhere, at any time, were any important objectives gained. Neither side achieved their aim of driving the invading enemy into the sea (the Turks), or getting anywhere near taking the hilly, strategic prize of Achi Baba (the Allies). And yet the inconclusive, repetitive snails-pace continued throughout. The increasingly clueless commanders grasped at any straw – General Hamilton became convinced that the reason the Allies had not succeeded was because a lack of ammunition. At the end of July he sent off a message to Kitchener pointing out how badly served he was in the matter of ammunition compared with the armies in France.

In London, The Dardanelles Committee met to consider the position and Hamilton's representation. Instead of ploughing more troops and ammunition to the cause, it was decided that a new landing on the enemy coast would unlock the stalemate. It was proposed that the Allies should land at Suvla Bay. Throughout Cumberland and Westmorland, families waited in agony for news of their husbands and sons. *The Times* carried a story on 31 July that was subsequently picked up by the *Cumberland News*. In it, suggestions were made about the new offensive:

> *The Dardanelles Committee met this week to discuss the latest situation at Gallipoli. It would appear that the frustration of the Allies in not making the progress hoped for has led to a change of offensive.*

Words like 'offensive' can not have done much to re-assure the county's readership as the piece was preceded by a list – spanning two columns – of dead and wounded local men. At least the folks back home had an inkling of what was about to happen; this is more than the soldiers themselves – they were kept in the dark until the moment came yet again when they would be ordered into battle.

Before this latest development however, Sergeant Curran and his colleagues were treated to a week of near-paradise. After the Battle of Gully Ravine, 1st Border was ordered back down to Gully Beach. There, they learned that they were being sent back to Lemnos for a well-earned rest. On 12 July, the men were comfortably established in a camp about two miles from

the port of Mudros. The relief of being away from the heat, the flies, the noise of battle, and the permanent stench must have been heavenly. It was also an opportunity for the men to write home and by this time – given the coverage the campaign was receiving – it was pointless dressing up the truth for the benefit of loved ones. Captain Archibald Ellis summed up the time he and his men had spent on Gallipoli:

Sergeant Jim Curran

When one looks back on the conditions under which we have been living, one can only feel surprised that the men stood it so well. Incessant work, whether in the fire trenches, support, or reserve, at all time of day and night, within easy range of the enemy's artillery and nearly always within rifle range, monotonous diet in which bully beef, plum and apple jam and hard tack recurred with nauseating frequency, living in hot and dusty trenches, the surrounding of which in many places can only be compared to an open cemetery, and last, but not least, masses of loathsome flies for ever busy from sunrise to sunset. With such conditions, it is really more a matter for wonder that so many were able to stick it out as they did, and the example set by the old hands in never-failing cheerfulness, instant readiness to take on any enterprise, however hazardous, was simply magnificent, and a tremendous factor in maintaining the high standard of efficiency which the Battalion has displayed throughout the arduous campaign.

Jim Curran was among twenty officers and 800 rank and file who returned to the peninsular on 28th and spent a further two weeks in the firing line back at Gully Ravine. On the night of 16 August, they embarked for Suvla Bay. (Little did the men know that back home, Cumberland had had its coast bombarded by German U-Boats that same day. There were no casualties in this only attack on the county during the war).

In theory, Suvla Bay was certainly an ideal place for a fresh attack. It had safe anchorage for the fleet, and had lightly defended, low undulating country, that led to the heights further inland. There was also a salt lake about a mile and a half directly behind the Suvla Bay beaches. The Anzacs attacked at the bay named after them while 25,000 British troops would go ashore at Suvla. By the time Curran and his colleagues from 1st Border arrived, the offensive had been in full swing for ten days – alas with much the same results of those at Cape Helles further down the peninsular over the previous three and a half months. Amid orders, countermanded orders, cancelled orders, changes of plans, and general misunderstandings between various headquarters, the offensive and the landings had both proved ineffectual and costly within days. (The 6th Battalion of the Border Regiment – part of Kitchener's New Army – were among those landed at Suvla on 6 August). The arrival of 1st Border was also fairly inauspicious: after a confused disembarkation the soldiers turned to see their lighter – complete with the Battalion's baggage and supplies – filling with water and glugging its way to the bottom of the bay.

Once ashore however, the Border men noticed a different atmosphere from Helles: there were no flies. Perhaps this was a good omen and this new offensive would signal the end to the campaign after all. This would prove to be the case for most of the soldiers – one way or another. The Battalion was ordered to a small valley about 300 yards north of 'A' Beach and told to dig in. At 8pm they were instructed to advance to the firing line and report to the 159th Brigade, where each Company would join a Regiment in the Brigade and help them to advance their firing line under the cover of darkness. But nothing was ever easy in this nonsensical campaign and chaos ensued, guides went missing and the men did not reach the 159th Brigade until 10:30pm.

Sergeant Curran and the other NCOs discovered upon their arrival that the trenches – less than 1,000 yards from the Turkish guns – they were being asked to occupy, had been badly constructed by the inexperienced 'New Army Battalions'. Their first task therefore was to drive their platoons through the night simply to construct some decent, secure, dug-outs. There they waited. On 19 August, Curran's colleague, Sergeant Syd Evans was struck down with suspected tuberculosis and was evacuated, eventually back to England. He would be spared the barbarous assault that was now less than 48 hours away.

The following morning, the colleagues Evans left behind found themselves on hills, a mile from 'A' Beach – for the third time in as many days, they were ordered to 'dig in'. They were preparing for a major assault – ordered by General Hamilton – on two key Turkish positions: Hill 70 (or Scimitar Hill) and Hill 60 on the south east of the Suvla plain.

On the morning of 21 August 1915, the men rose to find unseasonable fog, which obscured their objective. Sergeant Jim Curran waited with his men, as his commanding officer Captain Forbes-Robertson was summoned to Brigade HQ on Chocolate Hill at 10am for orders on how the battle was to be conducted. The plan was for the 86th Brigade to attack 'W' Hills and the 87th Brigade – including 1st Border – Scimitar Hill. This (it was suggested) would unlock the stalemate on the whole of the peninsular and allow the Allies to press on up the ridges towards Anafarta Sagir and secure occupation.

The defending Turks waited in the hills. Despite the fact that for the most part, they were illiterate conscripts from the country who fought simply because they were ordered to fight, their attitude during the whole campaign proved determined and admirable. They were defending their soil against the Christian invasion from the West and they had their faith and their priests with them in the trenches inciting them to fight in the name of Allah and the Prophet Mohammed. For many weeks they had been preparing for this day; they were rested and ready. Even the allied soldier developed a strange fellowship with his opponent, dubbing him half affectionately 'Johnny Turk'. One soldier confided in his diary:

> *The Turkish soldier was very highly regarded by all the men on our side.*
> *He was always a clean fighter, and one of the most courageous men in*
> *the world. We came to the conclusion that he was a very good bloke*
> *indeed; we had a lot of time for him.*

Sergeant Curran and his colleagues probably shared this view as they waited nervously for Forbes-Robertson to return, knowing the assault was imminent. Finally, as late as twelve noon the Commanding Officer returned and informed his platoon sergeants that an artillery bombardment was to start at 2pm and the attack on Scimitar Hill would follow 30 minutes later, led by the Kings Own Scottish Borderers and the Inniskillings, while 1st Border would follow the Irishmen in support. These hasty arrangements added to the men's disquiet, as no time was available to carry out meaningful reconnaissance. Was this another disaster waiting to happen?

At the appointed hour, like every other battle before it, the shell-fire commenced; but also like every other battle, problems immediately became apparent as too few missiles were reaching the Turkish trenches. Things quickly descended into chaotic farce as the shells only succeed in setting fire to the dry scrub, which added to the mist that came down, reducing visibility for the advancing infantry. At 2:45pm the Inniskillings were ordered forwarded. They were immediately showered with shrapnel fire. Within minutes Forbes-Robertson and the other Company Commanders from 1st Border were receiving calls on their field telephones to advance in support. Orders were hastily given to 'C' and 'D' Companies to advance, while Sergeant Curran and his colleagues in 'A' Company would follow, with half of 'B' Company, while the remainder were kept in reserve. At around 3:30pm Curran led No. 2 Platoon forward into the black acrid smoke that covered the open ground towards the foot of Scimitar Hill, unaware that the Irish regiment ahead of them were being decimated by the Turkish gunners on the high-ground.

By around four in the afternoon, Cumbrians and Irishmen (or what was left of them) were ineffectually scrapping for survival, side-by-side. 'C' Company were being mown down on the left of the advancing line. By 4:30pm it is clear that it's another fiasco. What is left of 'A' Company have become detached from the advance. Confusion reigns both on the front line and amongst the observing commanders. 22-year-old L/Cpl William Townly is given the unenviable task of 'runner', to and from the firing line with messages for Forbes-Robertson and the other Company Commanders (Townly was awarded the

Distinguished Conduct Medal for repeatedly delivering messages and returning to Battalion Headquarters with updates during the battle).

No 2 Platoon 'A' Company meanwhile had found some cover at the foot of the hill. It's thought that Sergeant Curran's platoon was reduced to little more than a couple of dozen men by this time. Lack of clear orders, lack of visibility and a distinct lack of men were all compounding Curran's problems. Mounted Yeomanry and the South Wales Borders both tried and failed to relieve the forces at the base of Scimitar Hill at this time. As the likes of the heroic Townly was running back and forward with messages and commands amid the deafening noise and poor visibility, his instructions – when passed from unit to unit – were gradually (and understandably) being confused, misinterpreted, diluted or embroidered, depending on the particular communication link.

At approximately 5pm, there appears to have been a command issued to what was left of 'A' Company to veer to the right of the Hill to distract the Turks who were still mauling 'C' Company on the left. As attempts were made to shout this message from man to man above the din of the battlefield however, it was subjected to the inevitable misunderstanding. Sergeant Curran and his men waited for the order amid the confused insanity; by the time it reached the front, the units there – including Curran's – believed the order to be '...the remaining platoons in 'A' Company to move to the left in support of 'C' Company.' Curran couldn't possibly have known the significance of the error from his position. His fate and those of his men were sealed.

Sergeant Curran made a final check of his equipment and prepared his men for the charge across the 50 or so yards of scrubland to join their colleagues in an advance on the left flank. If this were a Hollywood movie, we would be treated to the arty, super slow-motion image of the leading man running with his men to take the enemy position; and if he were shot, he would be catapulted into the air – arms flailing above his head as he looses his grip on his rifle, and the camera follows it poignantly as it drops serenely to earth. But this wasn't Hollywood and there were no special effects – just brutal, terrifying violence.

Sergeant Curran gave the order to go; within seconds of leaving their position, the remaining men of 2 Platoon 'A' Company ran headlong into a blizzard of small arms and machine gun fire. Every man was cut down – most were killed instantly; Jim Curran was at the vanguard of the assault and, like his colleagues, was almost instantly riddled throughout his upper body with bullet wounds, but was miraculously still alive.

Such bravery from the thousands and thousands of ordinary service personnel throughout the generations can only be marvelled at by those who have never been in such situations; it is said that the camaraderie built up amongst colleagues and a fear of 'letting your mates down' takes over in such circumstances. But surely even this is surpassed by the single minded determination of individuals who choose then go out into the field of battle to rescue fallen comrades who are incapable of helping themselves. Quarter Master Sergeant Albert Prosser of the 6th Battalion the Border Regiment was one such man.

At around 7pm, a fierce fire fight flared up again on the lower slope of Scimitar Hill. The scrubland again caught fire and many wounded were in danger of being burned to death. At this point Prosser took it upon himself to go out into No Man's Land and save his colleagues (he would later receive a Distinguish Conduct Medal for his actions). Repeatedly he went during the evening hours under heavy fire to bring back wounded men. It is unknown how long Jim Curran lay among the hundreds of bodies that were strewn around the battlefield but in the fading light, someone – possibly Prosser – did manage to get to him and carry him from the field in the fading light.

10
No-one is Exempt

THE attack on Scimitar Hill proved to be the last British offensive conducted at Gallipoli – it cost a further 5,000 Allied casualties. Of them, the Border Regiment had fourteen officers (including all the Company Commanders) wounded and Sergeant Jim Curran was one of 377 rank and file casualties (killed, wounded or missing). The 1st Battalion had been reduced to 300 all ranks after the battle.

To add to this latest disaster, the medical services simply could not cope with the number of casualties: most of the wounded lay on the beach in the blazing sun, and within range of the Turkish guns, for three days. Communication was poor, organised evacuation was non-existent, and men lay in excruciating pain as confusion reigned. Some casualties were man-handled through a crude evacuation chain, until they were eventually loaded onto any available vessel that could make the four hour journey to Lemnos. Others were loaded onto field ambulances to be taken the shorter – but bumpier – journey to the casualty clearing stations. Sergeant Curran received the latter treatment.

Once at the makeshift hospital, the details of each man and his wounds were recorded. Attempts were made to categorise each soldier as a light or serious case, but the numbers were simply overwhelming and the staff was reduced to treating each man the best they could in preparation for evacuation. Their efforts were as honourable, but as futile, as those of their colleagues on the battlefield.

For death was omnipresent at Gallipoli. No one was excused: officers, and rank and file; young boys caught up in the outbreak-jingoism were vulnerable, as were grizzled old warriors with years of experience. It didn't matter if you were a shop keeper from the Punjab, or a lawyer from Sydney; if you were a dock worker from Marseille, or a sheep farmer from Christchurch; a lackey from an East African colony, or a bricky's labourer from Carlisle, there was no escaping the unforgiving scythe of mortality.

On Wednesday, 1 September 1915, Jim Curran died – he was 36-years-old. Amid the groans of fellow anonymous heroes, and the unhygienic squalor and heat of the field hospital in some obscure corner of the world, he had miraculously survived over a week after being mortally wounded during the attack on Scimitar Hill on 21 August. Winston Churchill would later write that those who fought at Suvla Bay were amongst the bravest of the whole war. But no amount of gallant words could compensate for the sacrifice.

By the time of the August fighting, Gallipoli had already established a reputation throughout the Dominions. It was no longer the 'Constantinople Expedition' touted some short months earlier by the decision-makers in London – it was simply Gallipoli; a funny name that was repeated over and over in the newspapers and one that gave chills of horror to those who had loved ones serving and suffering there. By now, the British readership were all too aware that things had gone wrong from the get-go – and the agony of waiting for news from this particular front was palpable.

At No. 14 Simpson's Court, Caldewgate, Carlisle, it is not clear if Mary Ann Curran knew about her husband's wounds received in the Suvla offensive. She may well have done, as it took around a week for such news to travel back, although Jim was not listed as wounded in an ominous press report in the *Cumberland News* on 28 August, giving some inkling of the disaster that had taken place. The piece detailed the offensive at Suvla and carried the title, 'Further Costly Efforts Required.' As the report was being read in Carlisle, Jim was still fighting for his life on the Turkish peninsular.

Tuesday, 14 September was the first day of the trial of the two signalmen responsible for the Quintinshill railway disaster. Naturally, the local press was full of the story that had briefly dominated the headlines back in May. But little interest would be shown in the story in the Curran household. That morning, the news most feared – and yet regularly received – in thousands of households around the country came calling to Simpson's Court. Around mid-morning, there was a knock at the door; it is unclear as to whether it was mother or daughter who went through from the back kitchen to answer it, but upon opening the door, they were confronted with the portentous figure of the blue-uniformed postman holding a buff coloured envelope.

My grandfather (Neil) was too young to recall the scene but a slightly older contemporary of his had the horrific scene cruelly embossed on his young mind when he witnessed the same scenario. He recalled in later life that he was eight years old when the dreaded letter arrived informing the family of the death of his father. It was surely similar in all households:

> *It was on a Saturday morning and my mum was feeding us. The kid was in the high chair, when there was a hammering at the door. I remember*

*her slight annoyance at the disruption as she went to answer it. And
then I saw her opening the door and taking the letter. She tore it open,
she was nervous, her hands started shaking, then she read it and col-
lapsed on the floor. John the eldest boy, told me to go to Mrs. Lawson's
a neighbour of ours. So I went knocked at her door and said, 'Would you
comes please, my mum doesn't seem well.*

For the Currans, it was over. The agony of waiting, hoping and praying was
over. For others it went on. And for some, there was better news: on 24
September, 163 men wounded at Gallipoli arrived at Carlisle station and were
taken to the Infirmary. News of the men's arrival had leaked out days earlier
and crowds gathered at the station to cheer and applaud the heroes as they
were carried from the train; undignified and embarrassed. Many onlookers
loaned their vehicles to transport the men to hospital.

But for Mary Ann, the task begun of picking her family up and moving
began immediately. She had to now cope by herself in a man's world, something that would drive many in the same situation to the point of despair.
Many women were already weak through hunger and starvation, and the grief
endured by their loss tipped many over the edge – a contemporary survey
found that one in eight of war widows – over 31,000 died within a year of their
soldier husbands.

In the *Carlisle Journal* on 28 September, 3471 Sergeant James Curran of
No. 14 Simpson's Court was listed as 'Died of Wounds'. He was one of 21
names in that edition. Mary Ann also submitted a picture of her late husband
that was printed in the 'role of honour' of the *Cumberland News* later that
week.

In London, the Dardanelles Committee remained divided about the whole
disastrous campaign; another 45,000 men had fallen in the August battles. In
October General Ian Hamilton was recalled to London and effectively relieved
of his position. One of his subordinates, Lieutenant-General Sir William
Birdwood – who had crossed swords with Hamilton during the campaign for
his ambivalence about the Anzacs – was scathing as he watched him leave the
peninsular. He wrote:

*Hamilton should have taken much more personal charge and insisted on
things being done, and really taking command. He never did.*

Hamilton was succeeded by General Sir Charles Munroe. He visited
Gallipoli and came to the swift conclusion that just as in the Boer War, the

The Curran family, 1916.

British had fatally underestimated the enemy, and that the campaign should be abandoned and the peninsular evacuated. The bitter Winston Churchill – one of the architects of the campaign – sniped, 'He came, he saw, he capitulated.' His less subjective colleagues on the Dardanelles Committee however, concurred with Munroe and preparations began to clear the peninsular. The campaign had been a disaster of the first order. Jim was one of over 200,000 Allied casualties. Critics of the operation labelled those in command the worst in the British Army since the Crimean War.

Ironically, the evacuation was the most successful part of the expedition as – throughout its duration, between December 1915 and January 1916 – not a single man was lost. The masterpiece plan adopted every possible ruse to dupe the Turks into believing that things were normal: troops bathed and played games, reliefs and ration parties went on, automatic rifles fired sporadically along the empty trenches, as 120,000 men, thousands of animals and hundreds of guns were moved off the peninsular. After 259 days, the Allies finally succeeded in getting one over on the Turks who didn't realise that they were withdrawing; or perhaps they just didn't care and quietly watched the invaders leave.

Mary Ann Curran didn't care either – it was all too late for her and her children. It was her turn now to follow the path of early widowhood, suffered by both her mother and grandmother. She appears to have accepted this challenge with amazing practicality – almost expecting the worst by the time the news arrived. Not only did she submit the picture of her husband to the local newspaper, almost immediately upon hearing of Jim's death, but months later – once her new baby George was born – she surpassed even this tribute. In the early months of 1916, she decided to organise a family portrait. She dressed her children up in all their finery, took them down to the studio to have their picture taken. But that is not all she did because, in a brilliant tribute to her husband – something Queen Victoria would have been proud of, concerning her deceased Albert – Mary Ann utilised the state of the art technology of the day and had her husband's most recent photograph (which was the picture of him in uniform, taken shortly before he left for the Dardanelles) superimposed on to the family portrait.

She then got on with the task of raising her family, relying heavily on the assistance of her two eldest daughters, who looked after their younger brothers. She never did get round to christening her two youngest sons into the Catholic faith as her husband had instructed; this was probably due – not out of spite – but out of expediency, as something that had once appeared to be an important family issue, now paled into minor insignificance. Mary Ann was one of a great number of widows created by the Great War. It was their job to get on with life without their husbands, and in doing so, show some stoicism and generally accept their (admittedly less horrifying, but equally difficult) fates, much as their spouses had done.

In 1920 Mary Ann received a large box containing her husband's posthumously awarded medals. The so-called 'Trio' of the British War Medal, 1914-18 Star and the Victory Medal were accompanied by the large bronze memorial plaque that was ultimately issued to all next of kin of those who died during war. There was also a Memorial Scroll which read:

Let those who come after see to it that his name be not forgotten.

Postscript

GENERAL James Wolfe, Vice Admiral Horatio Nelson, Sergeant Jim Curran. Doesn't sound quite right does it? When Jim Curran fell, mortally wounded, on battlefields of Gallipoli – unlike the other two illustrious servicemen who suffered the same fate in their final campaigns – there was no national outpouring of grief; no regiments named in his honour, no columns, streets or pubs named after him, no historians (apart from this one) who grew to revere and admire him. He was simply another statistic: one of three quarters of a million British servicemen killed in action; victims of futile, unimaginative tactics employed by too many of their commanders who were all too ready to throw life away for a few yards of ground. In total 784 men from the Border Regiment were killed at Gallipoli; 1,252 others were wounded.

History is riddled with ifs, buts and maybes. The cruel irony in this case is that, if the war had not taken place, Jim would have left the army – having fulfiled his seven years' service – in the very month he was killed. His body was transported to, and laid to rest, in one of the military cemeteries in Alexandria, Egypt. Amid the hundreds of rows of those iconic white tablets is plot number F156 where he now lies, never growing old, unlike those of us who are left

The trio of medals received by Mary Ann in 1920.

to grow old; time not wearying him, and the years not condemning him. A corner of a foreign field that will be forever England.

When Winston Churchill and his cohorts conceived the campaign in the Dardanelles, they thought it would be a swift successful campaign that would barely register on the grand strategic scale of importance. Little did Churchill know that 52,000 Allied troops would perish in the bloody fiasco, and another 150,000 would be physically and mentally scarred by their experiences. In 1940, as Prime Minister, Churchill would deliver the most famous speech in British political history when he growled across the airwaves, 'We shall go on to the end... we shall fight on the seas and oceans... we shall defend our island, whatever the cost may be... we shall fight on the beaches, we shall fight on the landing grounds... we shall fight in the hills; we shall *never* surrender!' I wonder when he was writing those words if he thought about how the Turks had fought and done exactly that, almost 30 years earlier at Gallipoli.

The carnage also resulted in Turkey losing 250,000 men and a moving memorial was erected by the Turkish government in 1934 that read:

> *Those English, French, Australian, New Zealand and Indian heroes*
> *who shed blood on the soil of this country.*
> *Here you are in the soil of a friendly country*
> *Rest in peace.*
> *You are side by side and lying together with the Mehmetciks.*
> *You, the mothers who sent their sons to war from far away countries!*
> *Wipe away your tears. Your sons are lying on our bosom.*
> *They are at peace and they will rest in peace.*
> *After having lost their lives on this land*
> *They have become our sons as well.*

But the ripples of Gallipoli touched more than politicians and soldiers; they touched the hearts and souls of families thousands of miles away. It was very difficult for those back home to come to terms with the sudden loss; with no body to bury and little or no information on the circumstances of death; 'closure' was not a word used in its modern-day context during 1914-18, but whatever the equivalent was, there was no chance of it.

And death in service could of course mean utter poverty for the hero's family. Later in the war, the heartlessness of officialdom was summed up by the uncaring, chief buffoon Lord Kitchener, who stated in a Royal Warrant:

> *A pension or gratuity for the dependents of a deceased soldier shall not*
> *be granted as a right. It shall not be granted or continued when the*

applicant is proved to be unworthy of the award in the opinion of our army council; or unless this soldier's services, in their judgment, such as to justify the award.

The state had been quick to recruit a man to fight and paid little heed when he was killed; similarly, it had been quick to encourage women to do war work, but was much slower to recognise the consequences of bereavement and the need for childcare. For her part, Mary Ann Curran bore her loss with dignity and resilience. Women were paid a separation allowance, when their husbands were away, but this barely covered half of the family's expenditure, and this was certainly the case in Mary Ann's case, with eight children to raise. And of course, when her husband was killed for King and Empire, the allowance stopped and was replace by a pitifully low war widows' allowance. Mary Ann and her daughters Maggie and Lizzie had to work to supplement such a meagre income; and this injustice was compounded by the fact that they were generally paid only around half the rate that men received for doing the same job.

Mary Ann's hard life came to a premature end in September 1928. Her life had followed the pattern of her mother and grandmother: hard life, multiple children, early widowhood, and early death. After she died, the Curran children became a rather disparate bunch: some of the children remained in Carlisle, with, most notably, the by-now married Lizzie taking in and raising the two youngest boys – Neil, aged fourteen, and George, twelve – while a couple of the others moved away to London. Eleven years after their mother's passing, the Curran boys would be all called up to fight their own war.

Headstone in Egypt in memory of 3741 Sergeant J. Curran, Border Regiment, 1st September 1915.

WILLIE GRAHAM
1
Enter the Black Sheep

THERE'S always one, isn't there? You know what I mean – every family has one, sometimes every generation has one; that sort of Del-Boy figure: the loveable (or sometimes not so loveable) rogue; the ducker; the diver; the one who perpetrates every scam going, to make life better for himself; and if someone else gets trodden underfoot, well, that's their hard luck isn't it?

Step forward William George Graham.

Willie Graham's story begins in December 1886 when he was born to parents Robert and Annie. The Grahams lived on Byron Street, Caldewgate, coincidentally, within yards of the Currans on Henderson Square. Labourer Robert had married Annie Fletcher in 1880 and Willie was the second of three children, splitting Jane Ann (1884) and John James (1888). Although the Grahams and Currans did not know each other at this point, there is an interesting dichotomy when comparing the two: the Currans were ostensibly Irish Catholic immigrants, while the Grahams were classic Anglo Saxons, descended from Reiver stock. The irony was, of course, that the 1880 representatives of both families found that – in real terms – nationality, religion, and heritage all counted for very little; if you were working class and poor, you lived in the same streets, had the same diet and vied for the same jobs. Robert Graham duly did the latter, getting work at the hirings as a general, and later, railway labourer.

As we have seen, the city was dramatically increasing in population by the time of Willie's birth, and by his fourth birthday (1890) the number of inhabitants in the Border City had been confirmed as 40,000. With this increase came the inevitable need for more housing. The City Minutes from the turn of the century outline the urban growth that took place during the decade (see next page).

With this expansion came slightly more choice and freedom of movement around the city for the working classes. By 1890, 40-year-old Robert had moved his family out of Caldewgate across to South John Street. The street was officially in the ward of Botchergate, but to the whole city, the area in which it was situated was known as Wapping.

Today, your average Carlisean probably hasn't even heard of Wapping: a forgotten area with little known history such as other – almost romanticised – areas like Caldewgate or Shaddongate. But as recently as fifty years ago, the area that stretched from today's public baths on James Street down to Crown Street, and from the Citadel Station to the Caldew had a dozen or more streets that housed 200 families. And fifty years prior to that, the figure was nearer 300 as working class families went about their business in their own thriving community, which was built around St Stephen's Church and school. Iredale's Brewery provided work for many of Wapping's inhabitants, while most kept allotments – and some others kept pigs and hens – on the so called 'Bog Field' further up towards Currock.

Wapping was a close-knit community, where everyone knew – or was related to – everyone else. Take John Craik for example; three generations of Craik had lived in the area, without too much fuss or fanfare, but it was the unfortunate John Craik that had experienced his fair share of betrayal, scandal and tragedy around the time of the Grahams arrival in Wapping. Five years earlier on 19 December 1885 John had married a girl from the same street; Isabella Wilkin, who was also the daughter of John's boilermaker colleague William Wilkin. John and Isabella were destined to be the talk of

John and Isabella Craik, probably on their wedding day in 1885 (child unknown)

Wapping before the decade was out.

At the time of her marriage, Isabella was a reeler (working on a machine that twisted twine) in the cotton factory. But as the cotton industry declined, so did jobs, and Isabella found that, after recovering from the birth of her first child in 1887 (Benjamin, named after his paternal grandfather), there were no factory jobs left. Instead she found a position working as a servant for the affluent Ridley family, who were fated to carve out a favourable reputation for themselves deep into the twentieth century with their chemist and optician shops throughout Carlisle. But regardless of affluence, every family has skeletons in the cupboard and one of the Ridleys' came in the form of Isabella Craik. Whilst working for the family, she had caught the eye of one of the sons of the household and a brief affair ensued, which resulted in Isabella becoming pregnant.

Relations outside of marriage and illegitimacy were as common in the late nineteenth century, as they are today, but unlike today's matter-of-factness, one hundred years ago the subject remained altogether taboo. And when the liaison came between two people from different classes, acknowledgement of any relationship was completely unthinkable. (There was an overall illegitimacy rate of nine per cent in Britain at this time. Glasgow's medical officer of health reported that he feared that about eight per cent of poor children were infected with syphilis. About 200 per 1,000 infants failed to survive the first year of life in many of Britain's large industrial towns, and many that did, grew up with hollow chests and rickety limbs).

What drove Isabella to have an affair is unknown. It is believed however that Ridley was deadly serious about his feelings for her and wanted to salvage some 'honour' by asking Isabella to divorce John and marry him. But his parents would not hear of such a match with someone way below his station.

Year	New houses built	New streets created
1881	222	12
1882	55	None
1883	73	5
1884	110	None
1885	100	3
1886	88	None
1887	112	3
1888	111	None
1889	68	3
1890	107	3

Discussions, arguments and recriminations no doubt ensued during the months of the pregnancy, until, on 29 March 1889, a baby girl, Emma, was born. Humiliation was soon to turn to tragedy for Isabella, as she had developed an infection as a result of the pregnancy and died on 30 April 1889, the same day her daughter's birth was registered. On Friday, 3 May at 2:30pm, she was buried in an unmarked Rotation Grave (this included other bodies). Her wretchedly young life had lasted 27 years.

Strangely, her husband John appears not to have disowned the child completely, as he is listed as being the father on Emma's birth certificate. Honourable perhaps but that's where his acknowledgement appears to have ended: in 1891 he remarried and went on to have seven children with his second wife Mary. Significantly however, there was no place for Emma in the Craik household; as her biological father was shepherded away from the city and inevitable scandal, his uncle and aunt adopted the new-born. Jacob Ridley was an accountant and he and his wife Jessie, and her spinster sister Helen Bell between them would raise Emma into adulthood. When Jacob died in 1906, Jessie moved in 44 Crown Street (Helen lived at number 42) with her adopted daughter. Emma was destined to live there for almost 50 years.

The house itself was owned by Dowell's Timber Yard at the end of the street, who charged the widowed Jessie 4s/6d rent. Entering the house from the street outside, you found yourself in the one main room; walking through, on the rough sandstone flags covered with 'hooky' mats, the back kitchen led out into a communal yard that serviced nine other houses on Crown Street, South John Street and Currock Street. Within the yard were eight toilets in a block and a washing house that was also shared by all ten properties. Upstairs was one bedroom, where adults and children all slept.

In ordinary households such as this, a cauldron of stew would usually be warming on the fire. A sheep's head provided a meagre element of meat, while swedes, turnips and other root vegetables would be added where possible; potatoes were relatively expensive but allotments would provide green vegetables at various times of the year. There would always be bread and margarine or dripping, and honey and sugar would be used for sweetening.

Fruit was something of a rarity – an orange for the children at Christmas being the exception rather than the rule – but that wouldn't stop the Willie Grahams of this world foraging for themselves on their way home from school, picking blackberries and goose-gogs; and if their scavenging took them near the railway line, then bringing home a few pieces of coal for the fire wouldn't go amiss either.

A closer inspection of facilities and commercial premises in the area gives us an insight as to what daily life was like for the inhabitants. For many, it revolved around the church – bible classes, choir practice, Sunday School for the children; a Saturday night lantern slide show in the Church Hall, followed by broth and tatty pot for the adults.

One of the local institutions to keep the families going between pay days was a pawn broker on Water Street. Women would take their rings and good clothes to be pawned on a Monday and go back for them on the Friday when their husbands were paid (John Craik and Robert Graham would be earning around ten shillings at this time). And when the women themselves couldn't make it in person to the shop, a local character nicknamed 'Monday Mary' would be on hand to call door to door to take items to the broker's shop.

When Friday did come, the local shop-owners were well aware of its importance and were not slow to tempt the local residents with their wears – vendors would go round knocking on doors with baskets of pies and baked jacket potatoes and the local baker made vanilla slices and Eccles cakes, trying to entice purchases from families who had eaten bread all week. The other delicacy of the day for the masses of Wapping was provided by the Tripery on Water Street that also sold cow heads and pig's trotters. One resident later wrote about her childhood and the community spirit that existed:

Neighbours had a lot of time for one another. If a woman was ill, neighbours would do her washing. Some did not have a mangle. The local shop owner Mr. Barnes charged those a penny for the use of his. Some people baked their own bread and there was a local baker who would allow them to take in their own dough in tins and he would bake them in his ovens. There were several small grocers in Wapping but my mother would get most of her shopping in the town, buying food stuffs in bulk – a stone of peas, a sack of flour – because there was seven children to feed.

St Stephen's Church (photograph courtesy of Ashley Kendall).

Whereas it cannot be disputed that most working-class communities like those in Wapping generated a powerful sense of identity and shared values, they were by no means as crime-free as they appear in rosy retrospect. Drunkenness and its frequent concomitant wife-beating were common, and there was frequent violence, albeit on a small scale. Trouble in Wapping was not on the scale of the more densely populated Caldewgate, with its abundance of pubs, but it was not without its disturbances as some of the less public spirited inhabitants spent most of their spare time and money on fuelling up on XXX, the beer sold by the Iredale Brewery, before causing rowdiness in the streets. It seemed at times that the Green Templers, a temperance movement based in the Church Hall, were swimming against an unstoppable tide of depravity.

Nationally, the passing of Queen Victoria and the accession of her son Edward VII – the playboy who became king – had signalled a change, on a scale never before seen. Edward set about reforming the monarchy: he introduced showmanship and ceremonial that his mother had detested. His coronation in 1902 coincided with national rejoicing at the victorious outcome of the Boer War, and this coupled with the new century appeared to signal an end to stuffy Victorianism and dawning of celebratory Edwardianism. But this air of free spirit also awakened demons in the working populace who now sensed they had a greater opportunity than ever to influence and accelerate positive change on their terms; no longer would they simply conform to what officialdom dictated or what previous generations had put up with.

The year of the King's coronation also saw the Conservative government introduce a new Education Act that abolished all 2568 school boards and handed over their duties to local borough or county councils. It was the first move towards a new Local Authority that would become universally known parochially for generations to come as 'The Corporation'. Amongst other things the new Local Education Authorities were given powers to establish new secondary and technical schools as well as developing the existing system of elementary schools. Carlisle's City Minutes of 1902 detail the finances of the new authority:

> *The indebtedness of the town as a Municipal Corporation is £73,358, and as an Urban District Council £153,402, making a total of £226,760, as against which the Corporation are possessed of assets consisting of properties, rents &c, according to the last published abstract of accounts, of a value of £600,422*

But the new Act proved unpopular with many as increased taxes to pay for the reform simply stoked the fires of rebellion in supporters of the Liberal and (growing) Labour parties. Men started to be arrested and jailed for refusing to pay their school taxes.

The have-nots were clearly trying to achieve parity with the haves, and the demand for greater leisure facilities grew. In the final years of the old century, the French Lumiére brothers had screened their short film *La sortie des usines Lumiére* (Quitting Time at the Lumiére Factory). With it, the age of cinema was born, and for millions around the world, the film astonished and enchanted viewers who had never before seen images move across a screen. Throughout the next ten years, cinemas started to spring up all over Britain to herald a new entertainment age. In Carlisle, Her Majesty's Theatre on Lowther Street was soon to become the exciting setting for thousands from across the class spectrum, who queued at various times of the day to marvel at the flickering images of people like themselves going about their everyday business on the giant screen.

As society developed an increase in its recreational activities, sports teams emerged, and the desire to watch increased as Britain became a nation of non participating sportsmen. Association Football was now dominating the industrial north and Midlands, and was drawing large crowds; some opportunists at one local club sought to take advantage and expand their own club. At the end of the 1903-04 season, Shaddongate United had lost possession of the Cumberland Cup and had been stripped of the Cumberland Senior League title, after a dispute over postponed matches. At their forthcoming Annual General Meeting, feelings were running high amongst many supporters about the future of the club. It was standing room only at the Temperance Hall in Caldewgate on the night of Tuesday, 17 May 1904, for what turned out to be the most famous AGM in the club's history.

After Mr. J. C. Barling was voted in as chairman, a motion was tabled to change the name of Shaddongate United in order to attract more supporters and establish the club as a representative of the whole city. A long and heated debate took place regarding the proposal with several speakers – for and against – having their say. A vote was demanded from both sides – the result was three to one in favour of changing the name of the club: Carlisle United was born. (There is a popular myth that persists to this day that Shaddongate United amalgamated with Carlisle Red Rose, to form Carlisle United. In actual fact, United played Red Rose in the FA Cup of 1905-06. Carlisle Red Rose faded thereafter and disappeared before the decade was out).

Back in Wapping, Crown Street had its own form of entertainment with Algie's Circus that entertained the masses. Algie was the alter-ego clown of circus manager Albert Comley; born in Cardiff, he arrived in Carlisle via the North East in 1900 and successfully applied for planning permission to build his hipperdrome on the site of the Palace Theatre, next to Christ Church on Botchergate. The venture did not meet with universal approval as one disgruntled reader of the *Carlisle Journal* wrote:

> *Is it not an abomination that a circus should be planted down next to a church? It is enough to make the dead rise up in their graves with infinite wroth.*

But Algie's Hipperdrome did open and this entrepreneur would prove popular with the people of Carlisle who witnessed musical entertainment, jugglers, sketches, and sporting events. Algie was also an opportunist and somehow managed to secure a copy of the film of Queen Victoria's funeral on Monday, 4 February 1901 – a mere two days after the event. He hurriedly dispatched runners on the same afternoon to put up posters around the city advertising the event; that night the theatre was packed out.

Another masterstroke of Algie's was to invite the pioneering cinema-

The Goliah Inn, Wapping (photograph courtesy of Ashley Kendall)

tographer's Mitchell and Kenyon to film outside his circus-cum-theatre. Mitchell and Kenyon travelled the length and breadth of the country between 1900 and 1913 filming ordinary people going about their business, and these ordinary people were obviously fascinated by what they saw. When they came to Carlisle in December 1901, Mitchell and Kenyon filmed the spectacle of Algie's travelling circus as it passed over Victoria Viaduct and through Caldewgate. The two then filmed the crowd leaving Algie's Hipperdrome itself; the same crowd then paid to get back in to watch themselves leaving earlier! (These images are thought to be the earliest moving pictures taken of Carlisle). In December 1903 Algie moved his circus from Botchergate to Crown Street (and the corner of Collier Lane).

Willie Graham was now sixteen and seeking work at the hirings as a labourer. But when both his parents died within eighteen months of one another, by 1904, he found himself scratching round for work that would pay around ten shillings per week allowing him to find lodgings and some spare pennies for leisure activity, which already by this time involved the repeated lifting of a glass in the nearest ale house. The following year, those who weren't quite so lucky at the hirings found some support from the new local authorities which – under the Unemployed Workmen Act – set up a labour bureau 'to help unemployed people find work and finance the voluntary emigration of those out of work.' The Act also removed the disqualification for franchise of unemployed men (but significantly, not women).

The Secretary for the Carlisle Trades Council wasted no time in urging the Corporation to adopt the Act and establish a Labour Register; in November 1905, he wrote Local Authority calling for immediate implementation:

> ...for the purpose of aiding persons out of employment to find work, and also help workmen over time of trade, depression by giving direct employment whenever possible.

But immediacy has never been the watchword of local authorities and it was resolved that:

> ...the matter be referred to the Sub works Committee to consider and report thereon to an early meeting of the Committee, and in the meantime the Surveyor be instructed to employ as many men as possible in removing snow from the streets of the city.

By spring 1906 the Act had been fully implemented in Carlisle and a report was presented to the authorities that listed 463 applications to the unemployment register between November 1905 and February 1906. Of the 463 applicants, 291 were given employment at a total cost of £500/16s/8d. The others consisted of 38 painters who were referred to the Surveyor, and the remainder were listed as either 'undeserving or single men.' One of those single men was our very own Willie Graham and this was his first knock-back in this adult world, and one that would appear to have seen him thereafter adopt a philosophy that he would retain for the rest of his life – that of *Man look after thyself.*

2
What is Poverty?

FOR most of the previous 100 years, Carlisle had seen immigrants flock to the city to seek a better life. That effectively ceased with the passing of the Aliens Act in 1905. It was the first piece of immigration legislation in twentieth-century Britain; designed to define some groups of migrants as 'undesirable', thereby making entry to the United Kingdom discretionary, rather than automatic. Originally conceived by the floundering Conservative Government, it was passed because of fears of degenerating health and housing conditions in the East End of London, the cause of which was due – according to many in officialdom – as the large number of Russian and Polish Jews who had arrived in the East End after fleeing persecution in Tsarist Russia. The editor of the *Carlisle Journal* was damning in his assessment of the act in his observations in August of that year:

> *The government seem intent on burying their collective heads by pursuing trivial issues such as this. Whereas there may be a case for reducing the number of immigrants to the country, surely it would be a more prudent policy to concentrate on the inhabitants who are already here. Meaningful reform appears to be beyond the capabilities of this current government.*

The editor was reflecting the mood of the population as clamour for reform gathered pace. The act proved to be one of the last notable actions of the Conservative Government as a few months later they were destroyed by the Liberals in the 1906 General Election, who roared to power on a ticket of social reform. And one of those to suffer among the Conservative numbers was one of the great figures in Carlisle's early twentieth century history.

Claude Lowther had emerged as a local hero when he had won the parliamentary seat for Eskdale in north eastern Cumberland during the 'Khaki Election' of October 1900. Lowther already boasted an impressive *curriculum vitae* by this time: educated at Rugby School, he was a playwright; an honourary attaché to Spain; and a member of the Imperial Yeomanry during the Boer War, where he was (unsuccessfully) recommended for the Victoria Cross. But then in 1906 he found himself suffering as many local candidates do when national issues are uppermost in the minds of the electorate; he was defeated by the Liberal candidate Geoffrey Howard. Howard was one of over 200 new Liberal MPs; such was the margin of victory. Once the victory was secured, the new government led by Henry Campbell-Bannerman began introducing their wide ranging reforms after a Royal Commission on how the country's Poor Law provision should be altered, and by implementing the reforms outside of the Poor Law, the stigma attached to claiming relief was also removed.

But even in the early stages of their administration, the Liberals were feeling the increasing heat of the emerging Labour Party, and if the Liberals didn't quicken the pace of reform, then they risked loosing future votes to new the kids on the political block – with their ideology for Socialism which was increasing in popularity – and in so doing, they would hand the Commons back to the Conservatives.

Someone with a little less interest in the national scene at this time was Willie Graham, the twenty-year-old labourer from Carlisle. Willie – later described by one of his sons as a 'grafter who was never frightened of work – was already ducking and diving from one job to another, full in the knowledge that he was unlikely to receive any benefits from the authorities if he found himself out of work. In 1906 Willie found himself labouring on the railway, one of around 40 per cent of the city's work-force that benefited from the railway; the factories provided work for the majority of the remaining work-force. The paternalist factory culture of the late nineteenth century was gradually eroding however, as – throughout the north of England – workers were becoming less inclined to celebrate the anniversary of their employer, whose political colours they followed without question, and more inclined to follow the path of trade unionism.

Elsewhere in Cumberland and Westmorland, a combination of shipbuilding, mining, and steel and iron works accounted for the vast majority of the working populace. As the twentieth century progressed, all of those industries would be dogged by industrial disputes. In 1906, the newly elected government recognised the changing industrial landscape and set about introducing legislation to address some of the issues at hand. Within twelve months of the election the Trade Disputes Act was passed: this sought to protected unions from legal claims, such as a firm claiming economic damages due to workers withholding their labour. The Workmen's Compensation Act quickly followed which granted compensation for an injury sustained at work. As the Liberals pushed their reforms, the trade union movement and their representatives in parliament – the Labour Party – pushed the Liberals. Unless working and living conditions were improved, they claimed, there were genuine concerns that workers may turn to communism or rebellion.

This apparent growth of socialism appalled Claude Lowther. After his defeat at the 1906 election, Lowther campaigned with all the zeal of any Victorian Imperialist for the preservation of Empire; two years later, Lowther's crusade led to him becoming chairman of the Anti-Socialist Union. But such opposition didn't stop the Liberals from pressing with their social reforms: a children's charter and old age pensions were introduced (this was for the over 70s; single men and women would receive five shillings a week and married couples 7s/6d). On they went, looking to quicken the pace of reform; none more so than the Chancellor of the Exchequer, David Lloyd George, who realised there was further need from government to relieve distress amongst the under-classes. The *Carlisle Journal* picked up on a speech he made to the well-to-do in Swansea in October 1908.

> *What is poverty? Have you felt it yourselves? If not, you ought to thank God for having been spared the sufferings and its temptations... By poverty I mean real poverty, not the cutting down of your establishment, not the limitation of your luxuries. I mean the poverty of the man who does not know how long he can keep a roof over his head, and where he will turn to find a meal for the pinched and hungry little children who look to him for sustenance and protection. That is what unemployment means.*

But while the Liberal reforms were one of the most ambitious welfare reform programmes ever undertaken by a British Government, there were proving to be several limitations to the reforms they passed. For children, free school meals were not compulsory, so many did not benefit; for the elderly, life expectancy was only 55 so many people never lived long enough to receive a pension, and even when they did, some were refused pensions because the criteria was that individuals had to have been in work most of their life (although 'most of their life' was open to interpretation); the labour exchange programme was only managing to find part-time casual work for the hundreds of people looking for employment; and the poor had to pay National Insurance Contributions out of their wages and the 7s/6d was not enough to live on, while unemployment and sickness pay also only lasted for a limited time. And to cap it all free medical care was available to only a wage-earner, not the wife or children or grandparents and other relatives. And although the welfare schemes introduced by firms around the country were welcomed, resentment remained among the female work-force, as the extremely low wages paid to the women and girls continued during the early years of the Liberal administration.

Such confusion and unrest came to a head in 1909 when Lloyd George presented his budget to the House. It would become known as the 'People's Budget' and was be so radical in its content, it would lead to a constitutional crisis. Lloyd George argued that his budget would eliminate poverty, and while trying to get the Act passed he gave this speech outlining his reasons for supporting the reforms:

> *This is a war Budget. It is for raising money to wage implacable warfare against poverty and squalidness. I cannot help hoping and believing that before this generation has passed away, we shall have advanced a great step towards that good time, when poverty, and the wretchedness and human degradation which always follows in its camp, will be as remote to the people of this country as the wolves which once infested its forests.*

Classic wizardry from the Welsh orator, but when meat started to be put on the bones of how this was to be delivered, the Conservative opposition – already hostile to the reforms of the Liberal government – became outraged by the proposal. The money would come in part from a super-tax on high incomes and from capital gains on land sales. When the budget was passed to the Tory controlled House of Lords for approval, it was voted down, and when the Liberal government drew up legislation to take that power away from the Lords, not surprisingly in a turkeys-against-Christmas move, they voted that down too.

The Prime Minister Herbert Asquith told the King he wanted to create 250 new Liberal piers to gain control of the Lords and swing the vote. But Edward was not enthusiastic – he was determinedly opposed to an increase in democracy in Britain (and was a firm opponent of votes for women) and – with the 1910 election a matter of months away, he sided firmly with the opposition.

In Carlisle, one of the under-classes who Lloyd George apparently wanted to help was otherwise occupied at the time of the constitutional crisis. Willie Graham had met Emma Craik, the daughter of John and the deceased Isabella

Craik of Crown Street. Parentless Willie by now had moved to nearby Denton Holme, where he was renting a room on Westmorland Street. Emma was three years his junior and was following in her own mother's footsteps by working as a general servant, something that would generally pay even less than the niggardly sums her female peers received in the factories.

These were the very people Lloyd George was intending to aid. He was out on the stump, selling his budget and campaigning for the forthcoming election. When it arrived in January 1910, the electorate appeared to take the 'all that glitters is not gold attitude', as the Liberals – elected in a landslide some four years earlier – saw their massive majority greatly reduced, which effectively handed the balance of power to the Labour Party and the Irish Nationalist members, without whom, the government were helpless. Despite the resurgence of the Tories, Claude Lowther again stood in North Cumberland but was defeated in the January election.

Not put off by their poor showing at the election, the Liberals set about proposing the Parliament Bill, which threatened to abolish the Lords altogether and replace it with an elected upper house. But in May 1910 – in the middle of the battle for control of the Houses – King Edward died. The country turned its attention to this popular monarch who had succeeded in re-inventing himself in the eyes of his subjects after his accession in 1901.

On 13 May, the newspapers countrywide carried news of the proclamation of the new King, Edward's second son George V (his elder brother Clarence died in 1892). The new king's first task however was not to concern himself with the crisis in parliament but to concern himself with a crisis in industry, and in Cumberland in particular.

The crisis came from that arm of industry that has been perennial thorn in sides of various governments over the years: the mining industry. It was, at the time, central to the British (and Cumberland) economy; it employed over a million men, and its large exports were a crucial element in the country's foreign earnings. And these million men were not happy with their pay and conditions. Life in this dangerous industry was highlighted when Cumberland became the focus of the country's attention in May 1910.

At the start of the night shift on 11 May (the day after the king's accession) 143 men started work at the Wellington Colliery in Whitehaven. By eight o'clock that night, news filtered out and into the town of something seriously wrong. Rumours spread of an explosion, which had blocked one of the main seams of the pit. As the night wore on, and the faint light of dawn appeared, there was still no news and the worst began to be feared. Only six had managed to

Proclamation of George V in Carlisle in May 1910 (photograph courtesy of Ashley Kendall)

escape immediately after the explosion, leaving 137 men still unaccounted for.

A telegram was received from Buckingham Palace 'The King is greatly concerned on hearing of the serious accident at your colliery.' Minutes turned to hours, 24 hours in fact, and a conference was held at the pit top at nine o'clock the night following the explosion between the safety inspectors and colliery officials. It was decided to suspend rescue operations for two hours until a specialist rescue team arrived from Yorkshire. When they did arrive, they proceeded to enter the shaft with special breathing apparatus.

On reaching the bottom, they walked for almost three miles before stopping to set their equipment in front of the raging fire. After only twenty minutes, unable to stand the heat and fearing another explosion, the men reluctantly decided to turn back. With their return to the shaft top, the crowd of thousands who had gathered realised the inevitable. A decision was made to build a two-foot thick wall in the seam in an attempt to starve the oxygen of fire. On the Friday morning – in scenes that would become commonplace during a turbulent national strike 74 years later – large numbers of police officers moved across the gates to the pit to combat miners rushing through to continue their own rescue attempts. It was all so futile: all 137 men perished. It remains Cumbria's worst disaster.

In Parliament, James Kier Hardie, the founder of the Labour party, put

111

pressure on the Home Secretary over the Whitehaven disaster:

I give it as my opinion, based upon my practical experience as a miner, that at the time it was decided to wall up the mine, the miners were in all probability, still alive. The fire which imprisoned the miners, took place in what is known as "The Bottleneck" and apparently this was the only means of exit from the workings... I hope Mr Churchill is not more concerned about shielding the mine owner than he is about finding the truth.

But problems for Winston Churchill (the Home Secretary) and the industry worsened when, later that summer, another devastating explosion in a mine near Bolton cost the lives of no fewer than 320 men. The Liberal Parliament bill was defeated and a second general election was called in December 1910. Hasty campaigning started around the country, none more so than in Cumberland, where, amongst others, Claude Lowther hoped to regain his seat lost in 1906.

In Carlisle, as bitter exchanges took place across the dispatch box in Westminster, Willie Graham married Emma Craik on 28 June 1910. Ever the opportunist, Willie moved in with Emma and her adopted mother to 44 Crown Street, where, on New Year's Day 1911 their first child was born, a son named William Richard. (As we have seen, childbirth outside of marriage was as commonplace then, as it is today. Willie Graham would prove to be a man of his generation and he was not about to set any moral standards for others to follow). Shortly after moving back to Wapping, Willie found a job as a carter for £1 per week.

King George meanwhile turned his attention back to the pressing constitutional issues inherited from his father. He was proving more receptive than Edward to the Liberal's proposal to reign in the House of Lords but he wanted something in return. After months of consideration and negotiation, George proposed a you-scratch-my-back deal with the government to pass the budget, on the condition that the crown would stop paying any income tax. The deal was struck and the Parliament Act was introduced to severely cut back the powers of the upper house: from now on, whatever the elected government in the Commons decided to do, they could progress unhindered by the unelected Lords.

3

Suffering and Suffrage

TODAY, authorities, governments and any other body worth its salt fill their manifestoes with watchwords like 'equality and diversity,' 'community cohesion,' and 'democratic engagement.' But as recently as the Edwardian period, half of human society were used, abused and generally overlooked. This may have been a time of intense change but very few in authority were prepared to allow women to influence that change.

Less than 100 years ago, gender equality simply didn't exist; upon her marriage, a woman's property passed to her husband – and in return? In the eyes of the law, he could beat her, lock her away and generally treat her like a second class citizen, if that were at all possible amongst the austere lower classes – effectively, the man owned his wife. Similarly, any children were the sole property of the father, as the mother was not legally a parent. So when Willie married Emma Craik, both parties knew that once Emma's adopted mother Jessie died, Willie would automatically become the head of the house with rights to all the goods and chattels contained within. Within two years of Willie and Emma' marriage, Jessie did pass away, aged 68.

One of Emma's sons today describes his mother as a caring person who was a good cook and baker, and adding, without any intended facetiousness, 'mind you, she had to be with eleven kids.' (We will see little Grahams continually appear as Willie and Emma's story unfolds). He also added that Emma never attended school; this was not totally unusual as school boards struggled to enforce attendance around the turn of the century – especially in working class areas where female children it was felt were more useful in the home. Whether it is true or not in Emma's case, evidence that she was literate is provided on her wedding day when she signed her wedding certificate with a strong, steady hand.

This was well and truly a man's world. There were, of course, many kindly husbands who tempered their despotism with benevolence; there were also fathers who happily allowed their wives to have the final say in the household; but for the most part, all classes of Edwardian society was patriarchal. In many working class homes in the cities wives got up early to pack up a midday meal of their husbands; and every Friday night, a stream of women could be seen trooping into the nearest hostelry to wrestle the weekly wage from their spouse who – if left to his own devices – would quite happily drink away his salary. And for the women who were not strong or influential enough to rescue some money at the end of the week, they faced the spectre of the returning drunken husband, many of whom would think little of physically or sexually assaulting his wife, to satisfy his own urges.

Bizarrely, the one woman who had dominated most of the previous century, Queen Victoria, was herself, dead against women's rights. One right in particular was becoming a national issue as the nineteenth century drew to its close: that of suffrage – the right to vote. Initially, the woman's suffrage movement was one primarily run by working class women; women who were frustrated by their social and economic situation and sought for an outlet through which to initiate change. Although women's rights to suffrage had been championed by a few for some decades, the movement for women to have the vote really started in earnest in 1897 with Millicent Fawcett founded the National Union of Women's Suffrage. (Four years earlier New Zealand became the first country in the world to grant women over 21 the vote in parliamentary elections).

Millicent believed in peaceful protest. She firmly believed that any violence or trouble would be totally counter-productive and simply persuade men that women could not be trusted to vote. However, any progress made by Millicent and her dedicated colleagues was painfully slow. Emmeline Pankurst was one of the hundreds of angry women, frustrated by officialdom's attiture to their cause, which ranged from narrow-minded delaying tactics, to hostility and dismissiveness. In 1903 she founded the Women's Social and Political Union – it was time for action. Unlike Millicent, Emmeline, her daughters and her colleagues, were prepared to use violence to get what they wanted. The Union was dubbed by the *Daily Mail* the 'Suffragettes'. Emmeline wrote in her autobiography:

> ... *this was the beginning of a campaign the like of which was never known in England, or for that matter in any other country... we interrupted a great many meetings... and we were violently thrown out and insulted. Often we were painfully bruised and hurt.*

By the end of the decade, the Liberal Government's argument was that the suffragettes should not get the vote because they were too emotional and could not think the same as men. Their violent actions were used as evidence in support of this argument. This was exactly what Millicent Fawcett had warned against over ten years earlier.

Despite being attacked by a suffragette wielding whip in 1909, the Home Secretary Winston Churchill had been on principle, sympathetic to the cause of votes for women, not least because his beloved wife Clementine was a supporter. Things even looked at one point as though suffragettes could be placated as the Prime Minister Herbert Asquith proposed a 'Conciliation Bill', intended to enfranchise women property owners; but this then got the bogged down in red tape and the patience of Mrs. Pankhurst and her colleagues in the Women's Social and Political Union (WSPU), not unreasonably, ran out. The suffragettes were adding to an air of rebellion as the new decade dawned.

The union movement was growing and the lower classes were pressing for equality. Increasingly militant unions and heavy handed authorities were a recipe for disaster. On 8 November 1910 a serious riot broke out in Wales, in which a minor was killed and 60 shops looted. Never one for the subtle approach, Churchill sent troops to Tonypandy to brake up the resulting strikers. This, coupled with his declaration in parliament that he would not after all support the enfranchising of women, led Churchill and the Liberals to alienate themselves from the electorate still further. With another general election less than a month away, the *Carlisle Journal* summed up the mood of the city and the nation:

> *What is to become of our country? Insurgency appears to be taking over everywhere and the government appear unable or unwilling to stop it.*

Worse was to follow: on 21 November 1910, the Carlisle readership learned of more rebellion – this time in the heart of government itself. Since Churchill had not supported the suffragettes cause, Mrs. Pankhurst and her colleagues had, themselves turned to more militant action to get their message across. A demonstration was organised for Parliament Square on 18 November 1910. Churchill gave instruction to police not to arrest women, but, at the same time, not to allow them access to parliament. Thousands of women pushed hard against the police barrier. Pushing and shoving led to six hours of fighting and became known as 'Bloody Friday.' Shamefully, police beat up as many suffragettes as they could lay their hands on – instead of no arrests, there were in fact 250. Once in prison, the suffragettes went on hunger strike only to be brutally force-fed.

The second general election of 1910 came and went in December with little change to the results delivered earlier in the year. The one significant difference locally was that the popular Claude Lowther regained his North Cumberland seat. Joyous scenes took place in the centre of Carlisle as Lowther made his way to a reception at the Central Hotel. Nationally, the status quo remained: the Liberal Party did not have a majority in the House of Commons and so entered into a coalition with 42 Labour Party MPs who had been elected. The Liberals actually held 272 seats, only one more than the Conservatives. This led to further reforms as the Liberals required Labour and Irish support to remain in office. This allowed the Liberals to continue with their struggle to pass the Parliament bill; it also facilitated further social reform as the Labour Party were allied to workers through their affiliation to the burgeoning trade union movement. But it clearly wasn't enough as opponents and extremists increasingly demanded different legislation. The national political scene was a tinderbox waiting to explode.

The most important legislation delivered was once more associated with David Lloyd George. The National Insurance Act was accepted by Parliament. But if the opposition didn't get you, then it seemed the press would; the act was

Claude Lowther arrives in triumph at the Central Hotel (photograph courtesy of Ashley Kendall)

116

the subject of much hostile criticism in the press and was bitterly opposed by gentry. In August 1911, the Liberals finally succeeded in getting the Parliament Act passed; the act scraped through by 131 votes to 114 and the House of Lords saw its powers reduced for the first time in its 600 year history.

There was little time for rejoicing however as the government were faced with increasingly widespread industrial action, the beginning of which coincided with the passing of the Parliament Act in August 1911. First came the national railway strike that soon found its way to Cumberland. Violence erupted at Silloth and a riot broke out at the Citadel Station in Carlisle when striking workers were confronted by police. The local press quickly dubbed it 'strike fever.' There was more to follow.

On Thursday, 24 August 1911, the girls in the tin printing works at Hudson Scott's on James Street walked out in a demand for more pay. Management cleared the factory and locked the doors until the following Monday – the girls, and over 1,000 men went without pay. Undeterred, female workers at Carr's Biscuit Factory and Fusehill Hospital followed suit the following week.

Loyalties were becoming tested as the wave of strikes continued throughout the summer and autumn of 1911, as the working men (and women) were demonstrating unrest and were making claims that had seldom been made before. Trade unions became almost as unpopular with the rank and file as they were with capitalists as frustrations grew. Two years earlier, in an effort to improve the lot of those whose pay was regarded as extremely low the Trade Board Act had been introduced, predominantly to deal with 'sweated industries'. Significantly it did not include the tin box makers – hence the unrest at Hudson Scott's. Increasingly, the low paid workers felt that strike action was the only means by which they could get a wage increase.

In the same year as industrial action became commonplace, the Chancellor Lloyd George successfully proposed the two-part National Insurance Act, which laid the foundations of the modern welfare state. The first part of the act saw compulsory health insurance provided for workers earning less than £160 per year. The scheme was contributed to by the worker, who contributed four pennies, the employer who contributed three pennies, and the government who contributed two pennies, all of which entitled the worker to sick pay of ten shillings a week and free medical treatment in the event of absence; the medical treatment was provided by doctors who belonged to a panel in each district. Doctors received a fee from the insurance fund for each 'panel patient' they treated; for generations afterward, being off sick would be known colloquially as 'being on the panel.'

The second part of the Act dealt with unemployment insurance and was based on a similar three-way contribution scheme involving the worker, his employer and the government. It gave the worker the right to unemployment pay of 7s/6d a week for fifteen weeks in return for a payment of two and a half pennies a week. The salary for Members of Parliament was also raised to £400 per annum, meaning that it was much easier for working class people to stand for election. But this all did little in the short-term to placate the masses.

Carlisle continued to be representative of most towns and cities around the country. And a trade as modest and apparently insignificant as that of a carter was not exempt from the unrest. Willie Graham and his colleagues numbered around 130 and earned their living by simply driving horse-drawn carts from A to B, transporting materials such as coal and timber. In 1911 the carters joined the Gas Workers and General Labourers' Union, who successfully negotiated a pay increase with the Master Carters' Association: the carters would receive 22s for a single horse driver and 24s/6d for a double horse driver.

The extra money would be much appreciated by Willie and Emma who celebrated the birth of their first daughter, Hannah, on 21 May 1912. Ultimately, eleven children slept in one bedroom top to toe, while Willie and Emma slept on the pull-out bed-settee in the one room downstairs. But for now, while the numbers were low, parents and children shared the same room. One child of the period wrote in later life of the matter-of-factness in sharing a room with one's parents, and all that that entailed:

> *My brother Dan and I shared a bedroom with our parents. There were two metal beds with straw mattresses resting on thin metal slats... Dan and I slept in the same bed. We slept so close to our parents that we could touch them. The nearness of our bodies made us feel safe. I accepted my parents' love-making long before I understood it. It was as natural as somebody using the pisspot... It didn't disturb me, or confuse me, or revolt me. Like my father's deep snoring, I ignored it. Living in such a confined space meant everybody shared in everybody else's joys and sorrows.*

Willie supplemented his income in 1912 by following the lead of Jim Curran and many of their male peers by volunteering for service in the Territorial Army. Volunteering was commonplace in peace time amongst the working classes of the day; for many, the army provided better food, clothing, accommodation, drink, money, excitement, travel, women, and comradeship than they had been used to. For Willie's part, instead of joining the 3rd

Battalion Special Reserve, as Jim did, he opted for the slightly less onerous membership of the 4th (East Cumberland) Battalion of the Border Regiment Volunteers. Now he would have the opportunity of puzzling over how he could spend an extra 1s/6d per day as a member of the TA. (We can only assume he found a way).

Facilities were slowly improving: like gas for lighting and cooking, water was now supplied municipally and delivered through taps directly into the sinks instead of through an outdoor pump. Water closets were fast replacing earth closets, and dung-heaps and human waste was removed though the town sewers, although shared lavatories remained outdoors. But whatever improvements were being made to home and work, the pace of change was proving too slow for the impatient populace, as social and industrial unrest continued. By 1913 – despite labour exchanges putting around 3,000 into work each day – the Liberal programme for the renewal of Britain, along with its own power base, seemed to be unraveling fast. One commentator described it as 'an obtuse exercise in self-destruction.' And like every government that gets into trouble, things went from bad to worse for the Liberals in 1913.

The suffragettes were becoming more and more extreme in their efforts to gain the attention of the authorities. One of the most militant was Emily Wilding Davison who was constantly coming up with new tactics to take the women's guerrilla war into the heartland of the respectable classes and, if she could attract the attention of the sensationalist press, then all the better. Emily's various hair-brain stunts tragically culminated in an event that shocked the nation on 4 June 1913. She devised a plot to hijack the Epsom Derby by pinning a suffragette flag on the king's horse, *Anmer*, while the race was in progress!

As today, the Derby is one of the most famous sporting events in the world, and as the large crowd gathered on the downs to watch the fifteen horses race for the £6450 first prize, no one knew that the day would be remembered for drama of a different kind. Ms Davison positioned herself inside the rails at Tattenham Corner amongst other spectators; there she waited until the thundering hooves of the approaching horses could be heard. As the field rounded the corner, *Anmer* was off the pace running third from last; as the horse came into sight, Emily leaped out from behind the rails and appeared to reach up, apparently to snatch at the reins. *Anmer's* jockey, Herbert Jones was powerless to halt the sprinting thoroughbred in the split-second timing of the horror – the horse ploughed into the suffragette at full tilt bringing it, rider and protester to the ground in a sickening heap. Jones suffered mild concussion a fractured rib and a slightly bruised face; Davison was knocked unconscious – both were taken to hospital. Incredibly, *Anmer* suffered bruised shins and not only made a full recovery, but also returned to racing.

Emily Davison's actions proved totally counter-productive. Many men in authority simply asked the question – if this is what an educated woman does, what might a lesser educated woman do? How can they possibly be given the right to vote? The general public meanwhile appeared to be more concerned with the health of the horse and jockey, condemning Davison as a mentally ill fanatic. She never regained consciousness and died of her injuries four days later.

Enough was enough; Emily's actions proved a watershed moment as far as violent protest was concerned. Less than a week after the tragedy, Millicent Fawcett and her colleagues from the National Union of Women's Suffrage organised a peaceful pilgrimage to London to lobby for support and to denounce violence. The call received a remarkable degree of support from the towns and villages from around the country. A letter appeared in the *Cumberland News* on 14 June 1913 calling for local women to support the cause and join one of the seven routes leading to the capital.

On the morning of Wednesday, 18 June 1913, around fifty women from the city were joined at the Market Cross by colleagues from Wigton, Keswick and West Cumberland holding banners proclaiming 'Non-militant Pilgrimage'. At ten o'clock sharp the ladies stood dignified in front of the town hall and sang the national anthem prior to marching to the station and then on to London. Once there, they joined 10,000 women campaigning for the right to vote.

4

Call to Arms

ONE month after the dignified, non-militant protest at the Market Cross, came a rather undignified, extremely militant protest in Wapping; who was at the heart of it? Yes, you've guessed it – our Willie. He and his fellow carters had met in March 1913 and instructed their union to make representation to the Master Carters' Association. There were six parts to their demands:

1. That 24s/6d be paid to single horse drivers
2. That 27s be paid to double horse drivers
3. That finishing times be changed to 1pm on Saturdays and 5:30pm on other days
4. That overtime be paid at a rate of 6d per hour
5. That no boys under fifteen should be allowed to drive carts
6. That pay to youths be on a sliding scale depending on age and skills

In the Graham household, interest in a pay rise intensified when Emma discovered she was pregnant again; but as always, negotiations became protracted and things came to a head in July 1913, when the carters lost patience and went on strike. Pickets were out in force in Botchergate and several unsavoury incidents took place involving pickets, police and bystanders – one saw a bulldog let loose and a near-riot ensued; a policemen managed to fell the out-of-control dog with his truncheon and the disturbance ended as everyone gasped in horror as when one of the pickets took out a knife and stabbed the animal. The crowd dispersed but more of the same followed a day later.

William Baty, who ran the Botcherby Brickworks, lit the blue touch paper when he hired a traction engine to collect a load of coal for the Crown Street depot and fetch it to the brickworks. This was normally carters' work and word soon got out among the workers as to what was happening. By the time the driver had reached Wapping, Willie and his colleagues were waiting in force. The hostile crowd jeered their derision and threw stones at the vehicle and its driver; unperturbed, the driver loaded up and set about the return journey, only for the carters to follow him. As they processed along Warwick Road, the crowd grew bigger and – if it were possible – angrier. Finally, as the vehicle halted, the members of the mob managed to release the pins of the wagon and – to loud cheers – the load of coal spilled out all over the road. It was a typical episode of the period; whether it was Carlisle or Glasgow, Bristol or Leeds, growing trade unionism had led to massive strike action all over the country. Winston Churchill later wrote that this industrial unrest would have been without precedent in the autumn of 1914, had other matters not overtaken.

During much of the Edwardian period, hints that a major continental war was in the offing had been implicit through the combined scare and war mongering of imperial propaganda. Robert Badon Powell had formed his scout movement in 1908 urging them to 'Be Prepared', and three years later the National Service League produced a pamphlet reminding every young man in Britain that he alone stood between 'his mother, sister or sweetheart and the inconceivable infamy of the alien invasion.'

But many could be forgiven for taking their eye off the various European machinations in the late summer of 1914 as war looked more likely in Ireland than on the continent. In March of that year there had been a mass resignation of British Army Officers based at the Curragh Camp in County Kildare. Their resignations came after being ordered to Ulster to deal with the potential threat of violence from the Ulster Volunteers should the Home Rule Bill be passed in the British Parliament. As most of the officers were themselves Irish unionists, they chose not to and the incident became known as the Curragh Mutiny. The uncomfortable year rumbled on with the events at the Curragh fuelling unionist confidence and convincing nationalists that they could not expect support from the British Army in Ireland. But events overtook everyone and Ireland paled into insignificance by comparison.

On mainland Europe – one by one – the complex web of treaties signed by each country to pledge support to each other, one way or another, in the event of war, were being triggered; the whole continent was being dragged into conflict. The alliances were supposed to be a massive deterrent, but only succeeded in guaranteeing the very thing they were designed to prevent: global warfare on an unimaginable scale. As German troops marched through Belgium in early August, Britain was dragged into the continental catastrophe through her 1839 agreement that guaranteed Belgium's neutrality in the event of European conflict. The danger was now clear and present, and extra men would be required to deal with it.

The 1908 army reforms had seen a shake up of the Territorial Force, specifically designed to provide a trained, numerous, organised force in times of war. The regulars would fight abroad, and be supplemented where necessary by the Special Reserve, while the volunteer battalions – including Willie Graham of the 4th (Territorial) Battalion of the Border Regiment – would provide home defence. Regulars and volunteers may have been well trained but numbers were extremely small when compared with Germany who, within a week of mobilisation, had 3.8 million men under arms.

Lord Kitchener, the new Secretary of State for War, had little faith in the prowess of the Territorial Force; to counter the German numbers he believed new citizens' army would be required, made up of volunteers. He decided to create an entirely New Army of 100,000 men. Each man would be between nineteen and thirty years old and would sign up for three years or the duration of the war, whichever was shorter, and would agree to being sent to serve anywhere. On 6 August, Parliament sanctioned an increase of 500,000 men of all ranks in the Regular Army. Army Order 324, specified that six new Divisions would be created, collectively called Kitchener's Army or K1; it detailed how the new infantry battalions would be given numbers consecutive to the existing Battalions of their regiment, but with the addition of the word 'Service' after the unit number.

As with all pre-war hype, jingoism was rife: patriots and pamphleteers appeared on every street corner, calling men to do their duty; the iconic poster of Kitchener with his scary moustache, pointing his finger at you wherever you went, started to appear claiming 'Your King and Country Need You.' The population responded immediately as a steady flow of men increased all over Britain; 6,000 men joined up over the war's first (Bank Holiday) weekend. So many men came forward that they had to be turned away. Three days later the King sanctioned an increase in the New Army numbers to half a million.

On the afternoon of Tuesday, 14 August, the Cumberland and Westmorland Territorial Force Association held a special meeting at the town hall in Penrith, to consider the best means of answering Kitchener's call for men (although Kitchener was dismissive of the territorials, he was, to a certain extent, reliant upon them to mobilise the civilian population). The association agreed that special recruiting areas should be set up to encourage every possible man to join; everywhere was listed in their minutes, from major industrial conurbations like Carlisle and Workington, to market towns like Brampton and Wigton, to small rural communities around Kirkby Lonsdale and Milnthorpe. It wasn't long before the supply of men far outweighed the availability of equipment with which to train them or uniform in which to cloth them; men would find themselves training in civilian clothes whilst trying to master arms-drill with broom-sticks in place of rifles. One soldier in the Border Regiment given the task of training the new recruits later wrote of the almost comical difficulties he faced:

> *There were at least 150 men, and this number increased every five minutes. Here were old men, young men, men of varying degrees of fatness, ex-soldiers, ex-militia men, ex-volunteers, tramps and a sprinkling of sleek-looking individuals who looked like shopkeepers. However, they were all keen and attentive, and although many of them had never been in the army before, they were all the stuff of which soldiers were made. The dear old Depot became very much overcrowded. Cumberland must have answered this first call splendidly, and we all felt like real comrades to each other.*

Kitchener's request for half a million men would be achieved by the end of the month. And the cause didn't end with the military: organisations began press campaigns urging civilians to help – the Carlisle Citizen's League and the Women's League both advertised for new members to get on board with the war effort. And Cumbrians were all too willing to respond to the call; such was the passion for service, men lied about their age to ensure they were taken on; many over-aged men claimed to be in their late thirties, and all under-age men called themselves eighteen. (But once in France, the over-age men did not mind adding on a few genuine years. James Burford, a collier and fitter with one of the Welsh regiments, was the oldest soldier of all. He gave the game away when he asked his commanding officer 'what this here arrangement is on the side of my rifle?' 'That's the safety catch,' replied the officer, 'didn't you do a musketry course at the depot?' 'No sir, I was a re-enlisted man, and I spent only a fortnight there. The old Lee-Metford didn't have no safety catch.' The officer asked him when he had last fired a rifle. 'In Egypt in 1882,' came the reply.

The famous Kitchener poster (image courtesy of the Imperial War Museum)

'Weren't you in the South African War?' asked the CO. 'No sir, I tried to re-enlist but they told me I was too old. My real age is 63.')

But for every ounce of romantic nationalistic pride, there is always a hefty dose of harsh reality for the populace, as the whole economy is steered towards supporting the war effort. Within days it seemed, everyone was affected by food shortages, reduced hours or unemployment; wages were going one way and inflation was going the other (during the first six months of the war prices rose by more than twenty per cent, while wages hardly moved). To try and correct this imbalance, the Prince of Wales set up a National Relief Fund, to try and give help to the needy; whilst locally the Carlisle Distress Fund was established for the same purpose. Within ten days of the war commencing, Sir Benjamin Scott, Carlisle's Deputy Mayor made an appeal for donations to either fund, inviting contributors to send monies directly to himself or make deposits at any of the city's banks. Scott's appeal was not without foundation – the *Cumberland News* painted a grim picture on 15 August 1914:

> *To a large extent, the war has detrimentally affected the ordinary affairs connected with local life. Many events have been cancelled. It is also taking its toll on industries and a major portion of the local workers are on short time. The food panic has fortunately passed but prices of provisions remain normal. Various measures are being taken to cope with distress throughout the country.*

News from the front was already grim and the British Expeditionary Force (as the army was dubbed) had experienced heavy losses as the Battle of Mons; on 28 August therefore, Kitchener asked for another 100,000 men to volunteer. Army Order 382 was issued on 11 September, specifying an additional six Divisions, which naturally would be called K2. They would be organised on the same basis as K1, and came under War Office control.

The number of civilians pouring into the recruiting offices was staggering; there was a patriotism everywhere that we perhaps don't understand today. Everyone had their own reason for enlisting: many were tempted by friends; others just followed their colleagues from work down to the recruiting office. Some workers that didn't follow the crowd had their hand forced anyway as 500,000 men were made redundant within weeks of the war breaking out, as industries shed employees in the face of economic uncertainty. For these men, many of whom would soon be hungry, the army at least guaranteed the bare essential of food, clothing and accommodation, so they joined too (pay was one shilling for a Private and 2s/4d for a Sergeant). And finally, if you didn't go willingly, there was the enormous peer pressure placed on every man to do his duty – twenty thousand women all signed up to an association committed to encouraging their men to fight.

Age limits were widened, improved procedures were developed, and partnership working amongst the various agencies involved, all helped the recruiting process to become that much slicker. On enlistment Army Form D 418A was completed by every man. After signature the form was dated and verified, stamped by the recruiting officer the same evening and sent to the Paymaster at the Record Office at the station of the man's unit.

Conscription – or 'Compulsion' as it was called – had been considered immediately by the government (Britain was the only major European country not to have conscription during peacetime) but due to response for volunteers, Prime Minister Asquith did not feel it was necessary to introduce it. The recruitment production line continued and places in the 2nd New Army (K2) quickly filled, so the War Office agreed to a 3rd and then a 4th New Army (naturally K3 and K4 respectively).

The 5th New Army (K5) was sanctioned before the year was out; what was significant about these latter armies is that they consisted of ostensibly locally raised units that in time became knows as Pals Battalions – men of the same trade, district and class, who liked to stick together and to be among the faces they knew. Lord Derby was the first to test the idea when he announced that he would try to raise a battalion in Liverpool, comprised solely of local men. Within days, Liverpool had enlisted enough men to form four battalions. This success prompted other towns and cities to follow suit – civic pride and community spirit attracted the greatest possible number of new recruits. God help you if you bucked the trend and didn't follow the queue, the shame associated with not signing up – even at this early stage – was immense.

Many were simply unfit for duty (incredibly around a third of candidates were turned away, which gives some insight to the poor living conditions at the time); but the ones who were pilloried mercilessly were the conscientious objectors, who refused to sign up on moral grounds. The social stigma for these men was great and 'conchies' were widely admonished and outcast.

The controversial Kitchener may have disliked and mistrusted the territorials, but many regular soldiers detested the idea of his new army. One, Sir Henry Wilson at GHQ wrote scathingly:

> *Under no circumstances can these mods take the field. Kitchener's ridiculous, preposterous army of 25 corps is the laughing stock of every soldier in Europe. It took the Germans forty years of indecent work to*

make an army of 25 corps with the aid of conscription. It will take us to all eternity to do the same.

In spite of Wilson's reservations, the recruitment snowball continued. The local MP Claude Lowther returned home to Sussex in September 1914 and received permission from the War Office to raise his own battalion of local men to join the Sussex Regiment – a battalion that became known as 'Lowther's Lambs'. Back in Cumberland meanwhile, the colourful Earl of Lonsdale financed and raised his own battalion to go to war against his erstwhile friend the Kaiser, who had visited the Earl on several occasions on his estate in Cumberland. Not unreasonably, the Earl decided to name the battalion after himself.

Not content with Kitchener's iconic poster to muster recruits, Lonsdale designed his own (in his own racing colours of red, yellow and white) and saturated both counties with it. The unsubtle wording left no one in any doubt about the Earl's enthusiasm for the campaign:

ARE YOU A MAN or ARE YOU A MOUSE?
Are you a man who will for ever be handed down to posterity as a Gallant Patriot? Or are you to be handed down to posterity as a rotter and a coward?
If you are a Man
NOW
Is your opportunity of proving it, and ENLIST at once and go to the nearest Recruiting Office.
REMEMBER
If you can get 15, 30, or 60 of your comrades to join you, you can all ENLIST together, remain, train, and fight together.
THE COUNTIES – CUMBERLAND AND WESTMORLAND HAVE ALWAYS BEEN CELEBRATED FOR THE FINEST MEN, THE GREATEST SPORTSMEN AND THE BEST SOLDIERS.
NOW IS YOUR OPPORTUNITY OF PROVING IT. HURRY UP!
Please take my humble advice before it is too late.
THE COUNTRY HAS NEVER BEEN IN GREATER PERIL.

LONSDALE, Lowther Castle

The Lonsdales became the 11th Battalion of the Border Regiment; by 22 November, 1153 had filed through their recruiting office on Devonshire Street in Carlisle and been sent up to Battalion Headquarters at Blackwell Camp.

Postcard advertising the training at Carlisle Racecourse (photograph courtesy of Ashley Kendall)

By the end of 1914, 1,186,337 men had enlisted in Kitchener's Army. Neither religion or socialism, nor the most pure pacifism was immune from the surge of this world-wide outburst of passion, and it wasn't long before the armies of the Empire's Great Dominions rose to hear the call to arms. 40,000 Canadians joined within a month; 20,000 Australians; 8,000 New Zealanders plus her navy (a higher proportion of any other Dominion); South Africans; Sub continentals: the Empire was at war. This is something that Germany had not catered for, or expected. But it wasn't long before these men off the street were receiving a reality tablet: the citizen army was soon travelling to replace regular soldiers who were being wiped out with alarming speed.

As for pre-war volunteers such as Willie Graham, they were considered to be in the army bag anyway and simply had to wait their turn to sign up, as enlisting officers struggled to process the tens of thousands of men who stood in line to join Kitchener's Army. Everywhere was gripped with excitement and nationalistic pride; no one knew that they were about to witness four of the most brutal years in history. But Willie remained patient and spent his days and any spare money he could conceal from Emma on his favourite pursuit – oh and that was another thing: having given birth to a daughter, Jessie, on 4 January 1914, Emma was expecting yet again.

5

Ammunition and Alcohol

COUNTRYWIDE, women's roles began to change. Even Emmeline Pankhurst instructed her Suffragettes to stop their campaign of violence and support the government in its war effort. Over 20,000 women took a pledge to persuade every man to fight and not to be seen in public with any man who was fit and free and yet had refused to respond to his country's call.

The work done by women over the next four years would prove vital to the ultimate success. They streamed into the industrial labour force, to replace the inevitable (and extremely serious) shortage of able-bodied men. The war would see many women and girls taking on many of the traditional male roles; this would, in turn lead to the authorities realising that women were capable of far more than they had previously been given credit for. Because females had, hitherto, tended to do part-time work and to work in smaller firms they had been less unionised than their male counterparts. Moreover, chauvinism was not only prevalent in government, but also the trade union movement was often hostile to female workers.

As the war progressed however, the scale of women's employment could no longer be denied and as feminist pressure increased – as did the levels of women left unmarried or widowed by the war – the views of unions and employers gradually changed as they were forced to deal with the issue of women's work (in 1914 only 357 thousand women were members of trade unions; as women-only unions were established, that figure would rise to 1,086 thousand by 1918).

Shamefully however, although women gradually gained acknowledgement of their skills, they never gained parity as far pay was concerned. The government had fixed wages but that did not stop unscrupulous employers circumvented wartime equal pay regulations by employing several low-paid women to replace one man, or by dividing skilled tasks into several less skilled stages. Through such deviousness, women could be employed at a lower wage and not said to be 'replacing' a man directly.

But such realisation of gender inequality did not register on many people's radar as Kitchener's new armies stood ready for action in the closing months of 1914. Eighteen hundred special trains had carried the British Expeditionary Force to its ports of embarkation in August; now a dozens more were whistling into Portsmouth and Southampton docks on a daily basis. There were some who were still under the misapprehension that it would be over by Christmas, but it was only just beginning. The nation may have been showing plenty of passion and commitment but it was totally unacquainted with the meaning of total war; the years of tranquil security were over and the British people were about to receive a brutally rude awakening.

In March 1915, the order was issued to create a Sixth New Army. In the same month Willie and Emma Graham celebrated the birth of their fourth child: a daughter they named Isabella (author's grandmother) – or Bell, as she would be known for the [almost] eighty years of her life. Bell's birth would not be the only significant change to Willie's life in this watershed year.

May 1915 was the month of the *Lusitania* and the Quintishill tragedies; it was also the month Jim Curran left Carlisle for the last time, bound for the Dardanelles and destined never to return. And as Jim left, in the first week of May 1915, Willie Graham finally received instruction to attend the castle to sign up as a member of the regular army. On 10 May, he attended his medical, where it was noted he stood five feet three inches tall and weighed twelve stone three pounds; his physical development and pulse rate were described as 'Good' and he was passed fit for service. Five days later on Saturday, 15 May 1915, the 27-year-old carter from Wapping became Private 21609 William George Graham of the 2nd Battalion, the Border Regiment. He signed up – as thousands of other citizens did – for 'Short Service, or the Duration of the War.'

Ominously, the day Willie joined the army, the *Cumberland News* carried a story about the Second Battle of Ypres, labelling it 'The Greatest Battle of the War so far.' The story probably passed Willie by as he had other things on his mind, but it was significant in as much as the bloodbaths at places such as Ypres were shaping his destiny – one that lay on the Western Front. Losses there were mounting alarmingly – 60,000 British casualties at the First Battle of Ypres (October-November 1914) another 40,000 at the second (April-May 1915); it was as difficult for the population then – in the early months of the war – to comprehend, as it still is for us today.

People had been brought up with their parents telling them about the seemingly endless Victorian campaigns where armies left Britain, went off to war in a blaze of pomp and circumstance, gave the opposition a good hiding prior to returning home in glory. Such romantic mythology may have bought the authorities a bit of time during the first few months of the war, but by the middle of 1915 the mood had changed.

For the first time, people were starting to question the war: its motives and its cost – both in financial terms and in loss of life – not to mention the length of time it was taking to win the damn thing; Christmas had been, and long gone, and yet here we were, no further forward and no end in sight. There had been greater progress in making the public and the working class in particular more aware of the empire and they in turn had responded to the strident patriotic slogan headlines whipped up by the press. But now things were different; before the month was out, the *Cumberland News* was representative of newspapers countrywide when it carried a story with the banner headline 'Compulsion Coming.' National disquiet culminated in the so-called Shell Crisis that came to the people's attention in the same month as the *Cumberland News* story.

The war was simply not going as planned, and the British press was there to make sure the British public knew about. Earlier in the year, Kitchener had yielded to political pressure and acquiesced to six newspaper reporters going to the Western Front. Writing under a pool system for publication in the national press, the stories ultimately filtered into the provinces. Initially the accounts were subject to multiple layers of censorship in France and Britain, so the reporters were never in a position to criticise the conduct of military operations, or even to report them very accurately. But all that changed when – after the failure of the Battle of Neuve Chapelle in March 1915, the British Commander-in-Chief Field Marshal Sir John French mentioned to *The Times* war correspondent, Charles Court Repington – himself a former soldier – that the allies had lost the battle due to a lack of shells. The story was reported back to the Home Front by *The Times*, which described the scandal in graphic detail in May 1915:

> *We had not sufficient high explosives to lower the enemy's parapets to the ground... The want of an unlimited supply of high explosives was a fatal bar to our success.*

This clearly pointed the finger of blame at the government and the Shell Crisis – almost overnight – led to a weakening of public opinion; the feeling was now that our lads were signing up to go overseas to fight while the production of artillery shells for use by the army was inadequate. Feeling the increasing political heat, the Liberals under Prime Minister Herbert Asquith formed a new coalition government with the Conservatives (thus ending the last ever Liberal government in the UK); David Lloyd George was given a new job as Minister of Munitions, as the government conceded that the whole economy would have to be geared towards the war if the Allies prevailed on the Western Front. Lloyd George immediately implemented the Imperial Munitions Board and reorganised supplies and factories throughout the Commonwealth, in order to supply adequate shells and other materials for the remainder of the war effort. A huge munitions factory was planned at Gretna to produce cordite, or 'Devil's porridge' as it would become known.

His Majesty's Factory, Gretna was ultimately the biggest munitions factory in the Empire, straddling the Scottish/English border; stretching some twelve miles from Mossband near Longtown, in the east, to Dornock and Eastriggs in the west. The mammoth site consisted of four production sites, two townships and an independent water supply – drawn from the River Esk – with a system consisting of a reservoir and filters, and several water pumping stations. To build it and staff it, 30,000 navvies and migrant workers (mainly Irish) flooded into the area as wages in the factory were disproportionately high compared with other war-time employment. With money in their pocket and little to do in Gretna, the workers didn't take long to identify nearby Carlisle as a likely location for after-dark entertainment. In turn, it didn't take long before the thousands of navvies were causing concern amongst some in Carliseans. One wrote:

> *The spectacle of stupefied men, often turn violent by their nightly excesses can only offend the ordinary and decent folk of this unfortunate town. But the spectacle of healthy young women rendered senseless by their manifest depravity, can only be described as obscene. On Saturday nights, this ancient town reminds one of those debauched citadels of the Old Testament – those on which the Lord reeks terrible vengeance.*

It wasn't long either before some of the issues were being reported back to Westminster, which prompted David Lloyd George – a temperance supporter himself – to later comment that:

> *Drunkenness amongst the dockyard and munitions workers was doing more damage in the war than all the German soldiers put together.*

Ammunition and alcohol were proving to be (not surprisingly) an explosive cocktail. The government may have addressed the first issue by building the factory at Gretna but if action wasn't taken to address the second, then their efforts to supply troops at the front would be completely negated; ammunition shortages were now being attributed to high absenteeism rates amongst drunken munitions workers, while profiteering breweries were standing by and reaping the benefits from their customers and their abundant disposable income.

Lloyd George was a man on a mission and he headed up a twelve-man government quango under the auspices of the Defence of the Realm Act, tasked the group with coming up with a solution to the 'Carlisle problem'. The newly titled Liquor Central Control Board decided that the solution to the problem was to introduce a unique social 'experiment' that would, they hoped, change people's drinking habits. The experiment would see the production, distribution and sale of alcoholic drinks controlled by the state. If the state bought and ran Carlisle's pubs under a strict code of conduct, he argued, then moderate drinking in pleasant, clean surroundings – preferably accompanied by a meal – would encourage a culture change amongst the patrons. That was the plan anyway.

A bill that set up The Central Control Board (Liquor Traffic) received the Royal Assent on 19 May 1915 – the same week that Willie Graham joined the army. What Willie and his contemporaries (and subsequent generations) would come to know as the State Management Scheme was born.

As the year went on, the scheme gathered momentum as the government put their full weight – and £225,000 – behind the Carlisle experiment. On 26 July 1915 the Board's first order came into operation, when the sale on drink in the cross-channel port of Newhaven – from where munitions were constantly sent to France – was restricted; pubs in Carlisle then started to be compulsorily purchased (all would be bought, along with four breweries by the end of 1916); and on 22 November drink restrictions applying to Carlisle were spread to other Border areas to stop munitions workers finding alternative arrangements.

The Home Office employed men to run the pubs in Carlisle, while unannounced visits from Government inspectors several times a week ensured the new licensing laws were enforced. The new licensing laws included a limitation of opening hours to 11.30am to 3pm and 5.30pm to 10pm and a ban on the sale of beer to under-eighteens was imposed. Finally, in a reminder that the man ruled supreme, the act stated that 'women were not to be allowed to remain on the premises longer than necessary for obtaining reasonable refreshment.'

So three major happenings occurred in Willie's life in the third week in

May 1915: on 15th he joined the army, on 17th he registered the birth of his new born daughter, and on 19th the State Management Scheme was introduced. We can merely speculate as to which he gave the most importance. But whatever he thought – whether he liked it or not – he was forced to turn his attention to matters military. On 21 May he was assigned to the 3rd Battalion of the Border Regiment in preparation for training.

On Friday, 14 May (the day before Graham's enlistment) Lord Lonsdale had inspected his 11th Battalion at their Blackwell Camp at the Race Course, prior to them leaving the city. They were destined for France, via their brigade training camp in Shropshire. 1267 all ranks of the Lonsdales marched down Blackwell Road and Botchergate to the station. The following week, the camp prepared for its next intake of recruits as the enlisting, training, deployment cycle continued. Among the latest number was Private Willie Graham. Training proved intense for all new recruits and despite having three years experience as a volunteer, Private Graham had to go through the tried and tested sessions that somehow turn civilians into soldiers. The days quickly fell into a regular pattern:

08:45-09:45 Physical Drill
(which included 'Rapid individual rushing at 50 yards')
10.00-12.15 Trench Training
13:00-14:00 Bomb and grenade throwing and in the use of machine guns
14.00-15.00 Rifle bayonette fighting – objectives and methods of fire
15:00-16:00 Muscle training with musket.
('Instruction is given in Section 54, para 266 of Musketry Regulations')

During rifle training, infantrymen were trained to fire fifteen rounds per minute – this was known as the 'mad minute.' The machine gun training involved using the Vickers' ammunition belt, which is nine yards in length – hence the phrase, 'Give them the whole nine yards.' Soldiers were also given various pieces of literature such as the *Hints for Troops in Trenches Handout* which informed men that sentries would be an hour about and covered virtually everything else from building rifle racks to carrying water. And then there were the little gems of advice such as 'Keep feet dry!' The men were also inoculated against typhoid fever and small pox prior to leaving camp. And the time for leaving camp was drawing ever nearer as the forces in France were being depleted by the week.

The year was not only a watershed year for Willie Graham but also for his home city. Munitions and State Management both made the headlines in

Carlisle but in the same year, the city was created a county borough and became independent from the control of the county council (then referred to as the administrative county). And it wasn't long before the Corporation were coming under scrutiny from its citizens. Hitherto, the one crumb of comfort to the British public was that – unlike their counterparts on the continent – they were not experiencing the cost of war in terms of civilian lives lost; but that probably didn't register as their cost of living was rising fast, and the poorer you were, the more you were bound to feel it. In theory the increasing war output led to war prof-

Central Control Board Arms 1916 (photograph courtesy of Tullie House Museum & Art Gallery)

its for the factory owner and higher wages for the worker; in practice however-er, the rising price of food meant that the real value of wages fell by fifteen per cent. One disgruntled reader wrote to the *Carlisle Journal* in November 1915:

> *Who is going to help me? Bread last year was tuppence, three farthings, and is now four-pence hape'ny for two pound loaf. The price of meat for baking has doubled in price; those of the cheapest cuts for boiling have trebled. I hardly know how to make ends meat. I have five children and am expecting another in June- we are eating less, and have pawned much to make up prices before the war and now. But that can't go on.*

It could have been Emma Graham writing: she had a house full of kids and a husband in the army; his pay was small, as were any allowances for a wife and children. Any delay in payment saw Emma trace her mother's footsteps to the pawn shop on Water Street. Worse would follow if her husband was killed or mutilated in the country's service – this could mean no income and utter pover-ty for her and her children. And if like Emma, you had a bit of a n'er-do-well for a spouse, the uncertainty regarding finances remained constant. Willie's first military misdemeanour occurred on 28 September 1915 when he was fined six days' pay for being absent from the Depot. It would be the first of many blots on his copy book throughout his career and one which forced Emma to tighten the family purse-strings still further at this time of rising prices.

6

Preparing for History

TO try and compensate for the rising food prices, the nation's gardeners were feverishly answering the call to increase food production. The elderly, mothers, housewives and their children picked up their forks and spades in their thousands, as a million allotments and back gardens were cleared and prepared for producing food for the masses.

In December 1915, one wag wrote in *The Times,* 'They said it would be over by Christmas; in fairness to them, they didn't say which Christmas!' As the second of the war approached, it was clear that this was going to be a long haul for everyone concerned. Having suffered disasters at Neuve Chapelle, Second Ypres and Festubert, the army required a major review. Much of it was re-organised incorporating Regular Army units with locally-raised ones – the idea being that regulars would 'stiffen' the new army battalions. In practice even the original regular battalions had a large and increasing contingent of wartime volunteers who had replaced the losses among the professional soldiers. As part of the review, on 19 December 1915, a new Commander-in-Chief was also appointed to the British Expeditionary Force in France. Sir Douglas Haig would become one of the most infamous and controversial figures of the whole war. His mantra was total offense and any hope soldiers at the front and their families back home had of adopting a tactical, sensitive approach to the campaign were dispelled when Haig announced:

> *Every position must be held to the last man: there must be no retirement. With our backs to the wall, and believing in the justice of our cause, each one of us must fight on to the end.*

By the time these words of wisdom were uttered, there had been an equinox, as, for the first time, casualties at the front were outnumbering volunteers at home. The first three armies that fought on the Western Front – Old, New and Territorial – were all founded on voluntary recruiting; now it was time for the inevitable: conscription. The (first) Military Service Act was passed on 4

January 1916 and became law on 27January. All voluntary enlistment – even for the Territorial Army – ceased, and every male British subject between eighteen and 41 years of age was mandated to enlist for general service in any unit as directed by the military authorities. (Incredibly, 5,704,416 men – about a quarter of the adult male population of the United Kingdom – passed through the army at some point during the war. Just under half, 2,446,719, were volunteers, and the remainder were conscripted by of a series of Military Service Acts). For the majority, they were destined to serve on the Western Front, the 400-mile long frontier of trenches that ran from the North Sea in a south easterly direction to the Swiss border; 200 miles faced Belgium, 200 miles faced Germany.

One battalion destined for France was the 1st Battalion the Border Regiment. They had already suffered dreadful casualties during 1915 at Gallipoli; now, what was left of them was now to face another bloodbath. Upon their arrival in France, the battalion were due to receive recruits from Cumberland and Westmorland – among there number, Private Willie Graham.

It is said that your average soldier only (*only!*) saw six days' action for each year he served on the Western Front. The rest of the time was spent digging endless trenches, moving ammunition and supplies back and forth. Willie Graham was destined to see only one day's action during the whole of the four-year campaign; in truth, he probably only saw a few minutes of that particular day. But the day Private Graham witnessed became the most infamous day of the whole war.

The date in question was one of those that – throughout history – are instantly recognisable for their significance as to how the events that occurred on that day shaped the future of Britain and sometimes the world as a whole. If history were one long essay, these days would stand like giant punctuation marks, signalling the end of one epoch and the beginning of another, whilst suggesting that things will never quite be the same again. One example was 14 October 1066, when William, Duke of Normandy conquered the Saxon King Harold II on a field at Hastings, and changed the direction of English history; you simply quote the numbers 'ten sixty-six' and most people know what you are referring to. Another modern-day paradigm would be 11 September 2001 when we all watched our television screens in horror as thousands died in terrorist attacks on America; the simple words 'nine eleven' trigger images in our minds and an instant recollection of where we were on that fateful day.

And another such day – a seminal point of the First World War – was 1 July 1916; it is marked down as the costliest day in the history of the British Army and would become a byword used by subsequent generations for futile and indiscriminate slaughter, because 1 July 1916 was the first day of the Somme: the most infamous battle of this, or any other war. (Some things are simply meant to be: this most famous day turned out to be the middle day of the middle year of the war).

Prior to the battle, the area north of the River Somme had seen little action; it had been held by the British since the summer of 1915 but for almost a full year few actions of any note had taken place. It was regarded as relatively 'quiet sector'. Instead, the major action of early 1916 had taken place further south west at the town of Verdun between German and French forces. On 21 February 1916, the Germans launched an attack on Verdun and continued unabated during the spring. Villages and woods around Verdun had disappeared as the battlefield was turned into a lunar landscape. One French soldier wrote of the horrors:

> *These days of Verdun were foul: several times before our eyes they have rained the veil of hell. Our mission was to be crushed, Divisions followed each other and each day – before the enemy – we would set up a wall of corpses.*

Finally by June the German pressure began to slacken appreciably. To disperse the military strength of the Germans and thus relieve the strain on the French at Verdun, the allies conceived a plan for the British to open an attack on the Somme River. The Border Regiment formed part of the largest [allied] army ever prepared: 1.5 million men, four separate armies; 18 army corps; 58 divisions stood ready for the planned offensive. It was the first major offensive in which British soldiers, rather than the French, played the leading part – and it was the first in which the British Army volunteers, rather than regular soldiers, were the main victims.

What was left of the 1st Battalion arrived in France in March 1916, after being evacuated from Gallipoli two months earlier and having spent a period of rehabilitation and training in Egypt. They were joining their colleagues from the 2nd Battalion (they had been in France since October 1914), 1/5th Battalion Territorial Force (also October 1914), 7th (Service) Battalion (July 1915), 8th and 9th (Service) Battalions (September 1915), and the 11th (Service) Battalion, The Lonsdales (November 1915). In preparation for the Battle of the Somme, the British Army required increasing from 450,000 to 600,000 men. The Border Regiment was no exception to this – recruits were required from the Depot in Carlisle.

At the Depot meanwhile, one soldier was already making his mark among his superiors – for all the wrong reasons. Within four months of joining the army, Private William Graham had committed his first misdemeanour by disappearing from his point of duty for five days in September 1915. He managed to keep his nose clean through to Christmas but the New Year was barely three days old when he disappeared again for a two weeks – for this he was taken into custody, confined to barracks (CB) and forced to forfeit sixteen days' pay. The following month and Willie was at it again: he went missing whilst on active service (WOAS) at noon on 7 March and never surfaced again until 22 – another sixteen days pay lost. (Presumably, he spent some of his time at home during these periods of absence; if his wife and children appreciated this gesture, they certainly would not have appreciated the loss of income.)

Instead of being confined to barracks this time however, the Army was about to have its own back on the scallywag from Wapping. On the 24 March – the day after returning to the Depot, and his daughter Bell's first birthday – Willie was informed of his posting to France with immediate effect, to join the 1st Battalion on the Western Front. With barely the opportunity to return home to say his goodbyes (his Commanding Officer probably didn't allow this out of fear of him not returning). On 31 March 1916, Private Graham and his colleagues found themselves at the 4th Infantry Base Depot at Rouen; he was

Children queuing for war bonds at the Guild Hall (photograph courtesy of Ashley Kendall)

139

now in the main theatre of war.

The base was actually part of General Headquarters – a huge area stretching from Le Havre, the BEF's main port of entry, to Rouen and Etaples, and up to the Channel ports of Boulogne and Calais. Private Graham was one of thousands of men who passed through the deployment stations of Northern France on their way to and from the front. The lives of the men appeared so cheap, they barely merited mention – then or now. One officer – clearly saddened by what he witnessed – later wrote of this almost dehumanising process:

> *The man seemed to lose his identity as an individual. Divisions were swallowed up in Corps and Armies. From this point of the war, one seems to no longer regard death as individual. Reinforcements would arrive, one never knew their names, they disappeared so quickly through the dressing stations. The individual man was gone.*

The men were given briefings about the front, amongst which were lectures on personal hygiene and particularly Trench Foot. The party line was that Trench foot was caused by tight boots, tight puttees, or any other clothing calculated to interfere with the circulation of blood to the legs, or by going to sleep with wet boots. (Many veterans later claimed that wet boots did not matter – as long as a man warmed his feet at a brazier, or stamped until they were warm, he would take no harm).

The standard kit for a private soldier weighed around 60 pounds. If he had not got them already, Private Graham was issued with the following standard kit: greatcoat, mess tin and cover, shirt, pair of socks, soap, comb, knife, fork and spoon, toothbrush, cardigan, cap, pay book, identity disc, waterproof sheet, tin of grease, towel, hold all, razor and case, lather brush, field service dressing, respirator, spine protector, set of equipment, pair of laces, rifle and bayonette with cover, oil bottle, entrenching tool, rations, pick, shovel, periscope and 150 rounds of ammunition.

The renowned gallows humour of the British soldier is no new thing: to try and keep their spirits up, the men produced trench newspapers; the most notable was *The Wipers Times* (the modestly educated soldiers couldn't pronounce Ypres, so simply re-christened it Wipers). In its first edition its organiser placed the following satirical advert:

> *For Sale: cheap desirable residence, Climate Warm, fine. Splendid link close by, good shooting. Terms moderate. Owner going abroad. Apply Feddup. Gordon Farm, near Wipers.*

On 7 April Private Graham was back on the payroll of the British Army – two days later, it was ensured he would be earning his money, as he was deployed to join 1st Border; four days after that, on the 13th he joined the Battalion near the front line.

The life of a soldier on the front line is impossible for us to imagine. Food consisted of any combination of bully beef, bread, bacon, rum and bitter stewed tea sickly with sugar. His routine consisted of breakfast at eight o'clock in the morning, followed by a session cleaning the trench and having rifle inspection. After working all morning (usually digging more trenches), he would have lunch at twelve, then resume work from one till about six, when it was time for feeding again. Stand-to would be at dusk for about an hour, and between bouts of sleep, he would work all night and stand-to for an hour before dawn. Added to this general routine was sentry-duty: men would do two hour sentry spells then work two hours, then sleep two hours. At night, sentries were doubled, so working parties were thus reduced; the men were supervised by officers who were on duty all day and at three hourly intervals during the night. One soldier wrote of his misery:

> When you come out of the line, you did not get much of a physical rest, because you had to go on working parties up to the front line, of which the great secret was the last mile everything had to be carried by hand. And in some way or other, you had to get up to the front in silence, in darkness with food, ammunition, drinking water, duck boards, and worst of all, coils of barbed wire. This makes nonsense of so-called periods of rest.

And all the while, of course, they had to deal with the odd bombardment from the enemy in their trenches a few hundred yards away. Unless there was a mad-dash across No Man's Land in the offing, shell fire was the main cause of death and injury to the men in the trenches – it didn't matter the level of your piety, bravery or wherewithal, the shell just killed or maimed you (the men called the shells 'Coal Boxes' or 'Jack Johnsons' after the American boxer who was heavyweight champion at the time). When they exploded the trench would be filled with a blizzard of metal that caused horrible wounds: from tiny shards puncturing the body or exposing a chest, to jagged pieces several inches long that could cut a man's head or limb clean off. The psychological impact of such an event cannot be understated. How can we possibly begin to comprehend the experience of standing talking to someone one minute, and then being splattered by their body parts the next, as they were virtually atomised by an exploding shell.

Officers may have had a less laborious time than the men but they could be forgiven for being more nervous. They were proportionately twice as many neurasthenic cases among officers as men, and his expectancy of trench service before being killed or wounded was again twice as long as his subordinates. When battalions were given leave from the front they could retire behind the lines for a few days rest and recuperation. It is said that mixing with locals and seeing children playing in the French villages away from the front, boosted morale amongst the men who can't fail to have been struck by the absurd juxtaposition of people going about their business while a few miles away, all hell was breaking loose.

For the soldier who was looking for a little more than the quiet contemplative environment of rural Northern France, there were also adult-only activities available for him to escape the carnage of the front. The Red Lamp, for example, was a well-known army brothel, that – at ten francs per man – provided the women there with a regular and handsome income. Often, a queue of hundred-plus men could be seen waiting outside the door for there turn. It was readily acknowledged that the girls only needed to spend three weeks at the brothel before they could retire on their earnings! Again, it is easy today to be judgmental about the morality of such activity, but as one soldier wrote, 'A bath, clean clothes and a visit to the fleshpots of St Omer proved remarkably restorative.'

The danger here of course was less to do with morality and more to do with health and hygiene – venereal disease had long been the scourge of many an army. During the First World War, it is estimated that the admission rate of Australian and New Zealand troops was as high as 128 and 130 per 1,000 men, while British troops suffered 24 per 1,000 men. The British Army reported 416,891 hospital admissions for STIs (sexually transmitted infections) during the war. Strain on manpower and medicine was immense as an average stay in hospital for a syphilitic-ridden soldier would be around 50 days. Not unreasonably, soldiers who contracted STIs were obliged to declare it – their pay was stopped and marriages were often put at risk as wives back home were informed of their husband's ailment. The more melancholic soldier would spend any spare time in a bar or a café trying to drink his sorrows and fears away.

As the day approached the number of men steadily increased for the classic euphemistic 'big push.' Many of the old regulars had been sucked up and destroyed in the dismal battles of 1915 – the men of 1916 were the men who had responded to Lord Kitchener's famous appeal. Kitchener himself came to a shocking and watery end on 5 June 1916 when he was travelling to Russia on *HMS Hampshire*; the *Hampshire* stuck a German mine off the Orkney Islands and was sunk with virtually all hands. This was evidence that this war was indiscriminate and unforgiving – no one, from the civilian labourer to the cabinet minister was exempt from its all-encompassing shroud. Reactions to Kitchener's death were mixed; the public were stunned as they saw him as a strong leader to whom they looked for courage and inspiration; the danger was that once the individual was gone and the followers were left to their own devices, a lack of self belief and uncertainty would set in. Kitchener however, was not universally popular: his own cabinet colleagues gradually lost faith in him, and his passing was summed up for many for the editor of the *Manchester Guardian* who is said to have remarked, '...as for the old man, he could not have done better than to have gone down, as he was a great impediment lately.'

Back in France meanwhile, that other moustachioed lunatic General Douglas Haig, was putting the finishing touches to the new attack with the French General Joseph Joffre. The munitions programme back home was at last bearing fruit and the shells poured into France to maximise the effectiveness of the 4,338 British guns; the cunning plan was to use the guns to shower German lines for a week prior to massed infantry assaults on 29 June, 15 July and 1 August and 15 August. The time and the place were now known, the tempo of preparation accelerated, as the assembly of the British Army was nearing completion.

7

Hey Lads Hey!

FOR the genealogist, scrambling through archives for snippets of information on ordinary individuals is unavoidable; sadly, this is often time consuming and ultimately fruitless. On other occasions however, it can be rewarding and very occasionally, you just get plain lucky. Take the case of Willie Graham for example. Any researcher will tell you that the chances of finding service papers for a soldier from World War One are slim, due to the fact that the building in which they were held was bombed and burnt during World War Two. So many records were lost that, statistically, there is only a one in six chance of finding the information you are looking for. When you are looking for a private soldier with a name as common as Graham, the odds are reduced still further.

When my researcher – a man with twenty years experience – discovered Willie Graham's 23 A3 sheets of information, you can imagine my delight and his surprise (he said he had never witnessed such a find before for a private soldier from WW1). What makes the find all the more amazing is that your average soldier didn't usually accumulate so much information; then again, your average soldier didn't get himself into as many scrapes as our Willie – the archetypal ducker, diver and general rule-breaker. Reading the papers seem to confirm the family perception that Graham was a character that didn't care much about anyone else and wasn't too bothered about officialdom. Mind you, if it wasn't for these papers, his exploits and mere presence on the hellish Western Front during 1915 would never have been known either; his own children (at least those who survived into old age themselves) were completely unaware of their father's experiences.

When you read about characters from the past – whether you are related or not – you tend to form an opinion or a feeling in favour or against an individual. I must confess to being a little ambivalent towards Willie Graham – he is not someone I particularly warm to. Having said that, he and I are very different individuals from very different times, and, as far as I am concerned, I am in awe of him because of this one event – an event in which I could never imagine myself. No doubt he, and many others like him, would have suggested the same thing prior to the war; many simply followed orders, many others simply didn't want to let their mates down.

Such was the tremendous amount of men gathered during spring 1916 they were split into four armies for the Somme offensive. General Haig gave command of the Fourth Army to General Sir Henry Rawlinson. Private Willie Graham was one of 750 men of the 1st Battalion, the Border Regiment who were part of Rawlinson's army; 1st Border was among representatives of 200 other regiments that made up the army of 150,000 men in all. The army's other siblings took the number of men to in excess of 750,000.

Upon arrival in France the men – incredibly for the first time on any front during the war – were issued with steel helmets, intended to reduce the number of head wounds (the helmets proved to be so effective that such wounds were reduced by 75 per cent). Remarkably, one divisional commander initially forbade his men from wearing them as he fear it would make them soft; it was this kind of decision-making that fuelled the perception that the generals on the Western Front were buffoons, way out of their depth.

In preparation for the assault, The Royal Flying Corps had won air superiority over the Germans and furnished their artillery colleagues with quality aerial photography. Below ground, meanwhile, sappers had burrowed their way towards the German lines and planted explosives that – when detonated – signaled the start of the attack. The preparation notwithstanding, General Haig acknowledged the difficulty of the task when he later wrote:

> The enemy's position was of a very formidable one. During two years preparation, they had spared no claim in rendering these defences impregnable. The first and second lines each consisted of deep trenches, well provided with bomb proof shelters and with numerous communication trenches. The front of each line was protected by wire entanglements, many of them in belts 40 yards long – with iron stakes, interlaced with barbed wire, as thick as a man's fist. The numerous woods and villages had been turned into veritable fortresses.

How much this was shared with the troops who stood on the brink that morning, is not clear. What the men were aware of was the unmistakable fact that the allied artillery pounded the German lines for the week prior to the attack – 1.6 million shells poured down, looking to soften up the enemy. Notwithstanding Haig's subsequent comments, he and his commanders were so confident that they ordered their troops to walk slowly towards the German lines – 'the men must not run or charge towards the enemy trenches under any circumstances.' But the week-long bombardment was double-edged because it gave the clear warning to the Germans that a major offensive was on the cards.

On 24 June 1916 Private Graham and his infantry colleagues who were to mount the attack in five days' time were billeted in the villages and hamlets behind the lines. A few miles up ahead, the bombardment of German lines commenced. The ear-splitting barrage continued as a noisy countdown to zero hour; the artillery would adopt a daily routine of firing shells for eighty minutes using every available gun. For the next four days, shells poured down on German positions, and gradually, so did the rain; the weather worsened as the week went on until finally – with the generals peering up at the sky like concerned cricket umpires – a decision was taken on 28 June (less than 24 hours before the infantry attack) that the ground offensive should be put back 48 hours to Saturday, 1 July at 7:30am.

So, during the late afternoon of Friday, 30 June, the men packed their kit, gathered in their units and prepared to march to the front. Regulations decreed that each fighting battalion would leave ten per cent of its number behind as they prepared for major conflict, to ensure that however bad things became, there would be something left of the unit. The soldiers and villagers who were left behind later wrote of the emotionally charged atmosphere: young boys – some of them at school less than a year ago – crying with fear as they marched into the unknown; colleagues – ordered to stay behind – racked with guilt; villagers waving and cheering, hoping that these men would drive out their occupiers. Four miles to the rear of where his men were facing almost certain slaughter, Sir Henry Rawlinson prepared a message for all the troops in his Fourth Army:

> *In wishing all ranks good luck, the Army Commander desires to impress on all the infantry units the supreme importance of helping one another and holding on tight to every yard of ground gained. The accurate and sustained fire of the artillery during the bombardment should greatly assist the task of the infantry.*

The soldiers fell silent – alone with their thoughts – as they marched the last few miles along the dusty French roads towards the trenches. One later wrote, 'The unspoken feeling of comradeship among us seemed to grow as we marched forward into a common danger.'

Upon arrival, the first task the men faced was to find their allotted positions; thousands crammed the narrow channels. As dusk fell, the cursing and shouting soldiers jostled each other as they moved back and forth to assume their station. With too many soldiers to cram into the front line trench, the support and communication trenches behind, had to be filled. Private Graham and his colleagues in the 1st Border found themselves in the support trench. When the order was given, they would climb out, move forward and lay bridges across the front line trench to get into No Man's Land. Once in position, the men were so tightly packed there was no room to lie down for what was going to be, at best, an extremely uncomfortable night; each had a rifle and bayonet, and a heavy back-pack which he was expected to wear in the attack. Most men leant against the side of the trench and each other to try and doze the night away.

Midnight passed – the waiting was excruciating. By 4am the first slivers of light appeared over the battlefield and the men prepared to go. Only at this point were some men told the time of the attack – 7:30am – up to that point they thought the attack would be before dawn under the cover of darkness. More waiting and greater disconcertion as the German artillery fire – which had been busy all night – began to intensify. The soldiers in the allied trenches had been led to believe the week-long bombardment of enemy positions would knock out most of the German guns. At 6:25am the British artillery started its daily retaliation. The previous days' bombardment had lasted until 7:45am; this morning would see it cease fifteen minutes earlier. It was hoped the Germans would stay in their dug outs expecting another fifteen minutes instead of manning their trenches – this would allow the British to take the initiative during

Local soldiers in a trench on the Somme, 1916 (photograph courtesy of Cumbria Military Museums)

the attack. That was the hope anyway.

At 7:20am the British barrage reached a crescendo as the gunners poured shells at the maximum possible rate into the German lines. Under this covering fire, some commanders sent out small groups of soldiers into No Man's

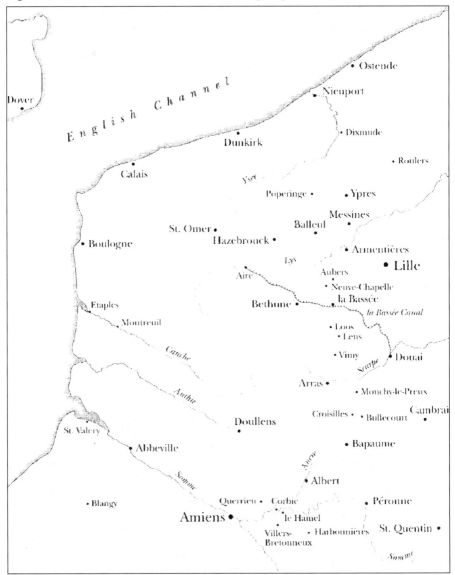

The Western Front: The British Sector (map courtesy of HarperCollins Publishers Ltd., © 2005, Richard Holmes)

Land to try and get as close to the German trenches as possible before zero hour. As the time ticked towards 7:28am the main salvo of mines were seconds from detonation – this allowed two minutes for the debris to settle before the infantry piled out of the trenches. With a blinding flash, the earth-shattering explosions turn the ground into a rolling wave and sent an earth column over 3,000 feet into the air like a giant black fountain. The only reason the men in the trenches remain standing is because they are packed so tightly.

At 7:29am on 1 July 1916, Private Graham stood on the fire-step in a trench on the Western Front, north of the River Somme; he was also standing on the precipice of history – not that he would have had any concept of this. Standing beside Willie were other local lads from all corners of Cumberland and Westmorland – volunteers who answered Kitchener's call to arms some months earlier. It is absurd and completely unjust to use words like *lucky* and *fortunate,* when referring to such a horrifying situation as Willie Graham faced that morning; but it is a truism that no matter what situation you find yourself in, there is always someone worse off than yourself. Some others who stood alongside Private Graham that July morning had been diverted to the Western Front after returning with the 1st Battalion from the horrors of Gallipoli. More fortunate than Sergeant Jim Curran in that they somehow survived that hell on earth that was the Dardanelles, only to find themselves in an equally terrifying situation; preparing as they were to go over the top as the seconds ticked towards zero hour. This had nothing of the pageantry of war associated (wrongly, it must be said) with the mid-nineteenth century conflicts.

Looking down at the muddy duck boards, soldiers gathered their thoughts. The battle was now in their hands; their generals could do nothing. Hearts thudded, stomachs churned; some soldiers shook with fear, some were heard crying, others stood numb. If it were possible to view the scene from above, 750 officers and men of the 1st Battalion, the Border Regiment could be seen; rising still further, you can see other parallel 'communication' and 'supervision' trenches, and then short connecting trenches every hundred yards linking these lines. The whole arrangement, covering perhaps 300 yards from front to rear formed the allied defensive system. Communication trenches were ideally long enough to permit troops to enter them without being observed directly from the German lines.

An ordinance survey style observation would reveal the same arrangement across a front of eighteen miles, with 750,000 men creating a sliver of khaki as they stood side by side waiting to rise from their trenches to assault the German lines; these men were Lord Kitchener's eager and enthusiastic volunteers, with hardly a county or city without representation. It was their first great battle. Further to the right, five French Divisions prepared to advance beside them.

The first task for Private Graham and his colleagues would be to get out of the trench itself. They were six feet deep and three and a half feet wide at the top, which enabled a man to walk along the bottom of the trench, on slatted wooden duck-board, with his head safely below the parapet. The parapet in the front trench sloped gently upward on the enemy side increasing the height of the trench, and making it extremely difficult to get out. They were framed with timber and iron. The men stood on the fire-step and rested their elbows on a narrow ledge in front with a row of sandbags supporting the lip of the parapet just in front. What were Willie's thoughts as the seconds ticked down? His wife and family? His misdemeanours? What he would do if he survived this insanity?

With 30 seconds to go, the most terrifying silence fell over the battlefield as hundreds of thousands of men froze in unbearable anticipation. Above them – in the clear blue sunlight sky – birds could be heard singing as they hovered and swooped over the trenches in complete incongruity to the scene about to be played out below them. Scores of commanders stood with whistles in dry mouths watching the second-hand move around the dial for the final time.

At precisely 7.30am high pitched whistles relayed along eighteen miles of Somme sector to signal the start of the attack – it was time to 'go over the top'. All along the front, thousands of British soldiers tried to clamber up ladders, scramble out of the trenches, pick their way through their own barbed wire, and then spread out into the straight line in accordance with the plan, before walking forwarded and getting what shelter they could. Of course, as we now know, the artillery bombardment had failed in taking out the enemy lines, and as the British troops appeared above ground, German machine guns fired up and the slaughter began. One soldier later described his experience of going over the top:

> Then five minutes to go, and then zero hour and all hell lets loose. There's our barrage, the German's barrage and over the top we go. As soon as you get over the top, fear has left you and its terror. You don't look, you see, you don't hear you listen. Your nose is filled with fumes of death; you taste the top of your mouth. Civilisation has dropped away.

Such was the intensity of the machine-gun fire; some men were hit as they attempted to leave the trench – their dead bodies gently sliding down the sloped parapet from whence they came. Others found their heavy packs snagged in their own barbed wire and were rendered helpless – unable to avoid the murderous machine gun fire from the opposing trenches, their dead bodies hung suspended in the mesh constructed to protect them.

If you managed to get out of the trench and through the barbed wire, then the task was to try and get in line with your platoon and slowly march forward across the several-hundred yards of bullet and shell-swept open ground. It's generally accepted that soldiers in warfare gain courage from their mates alongside them, and they, in turn, reciprocate by putting everything in to protect their friend or colleagues. But if you were a young soldier in No Man's Land at twenty-five-to-eight that morning, you were seeing your mates falling to your left and right, cut to pieces by the indiscriminate hosing from the opposing trenches; the whole area is already littered with limbs and bodies, and the screaming of the men is in itself torture. And yet, somehow you keep walking, waiting for your moment.

Incredibly, many British units did make it across No Man's Land but then found themselves en-meshed in the German barbed wire with the same result. But the thousand-strong waves of allied infantrymen kept coming; fighting took place to gain possession of the craters left by the mine explosions. The craters may have been still smoking and warm from the explosion less than half an hour earlier, but they gave valuable cover for attacking soldiers who could then prepare for the final push. When finally, some units made it into the enemy trenches – with blood boiling by this point, after seeing their mates slaughtered before their eyes – brutal hand-to-hand fighting ensued. The futility and brutality is summed up the [Border] Regimental diary, written on the day:

> *The advance just south of Beaumont, the objective being Bocol Redoubt; 2nd South Wales Borders who's objective were the first two German lines were wiped out with machine gun fire, in our own wire.*
>
> *1st Battalion went over the top from our support line, over the first line – the bridges over our front trench having been ranged from the (German) gunners the day previously. Met with heavy losses crossing the bridges and passing through the lanes cutting our wire.*
>
> *The men were absolutely magnificent and formed up as ordered, outside the trench and advanced at a slow walk out into No Man's Land as ordered. The advance was continued until only little groups of half a dozen men were left here and there.*
>
> *08.00 (half an hour after the whistles blew to start the offensive at 07.30) Advance brought entirely to a standstill.*
>
> *08.15 Enemy re-opened his bombardment on our trenches for which our guns retaliated.*

8

Carnage

IT is not certain how far Private Willie Graham got across No Man's Land before being hit. Like the thousands of others, he may have survived only a few seconds, perhaps a few minutes, almost certainly no more than half an hour. He received gun shot wounds to his left knee and thigh. Evidence to support the sooner-rather-than-later-theory comes when it is discovered that – unlike the majority who were wounded in No Man's Land – he received quick medical treatment. For those wounded further forward, there was little that could be done at this stage – they had to take cover in shell holes in the hot sun. Many would lay helpless for hours and simply bleed to death.

The medical services on the Somme were provided by the Royal Army Medical Corps (R.A.M.C.). Each battalion had a Medical Officer in a dug-out in the trenches along with a group of orderlies. This dug-out acted as the first-aid post and was used as an initial assessment area during battle. But within minutes of the Battle of the Somme, these areas were a horrendous mass of congestion and suffering; casualties were everywhere and medics had to work under the threat of shell fire levelling the trench while bullets from machine-guns whizzed by just overhead.

The more serious cases (and this meant virtually all the cases on the Somme) were evacuated to the nearest R.A.M.C. Field Ambulances. These ambulances were not the motor vehicles we associate the word with today (although they were also used on the day), but were static operational units behind the lines. With no facilities for surgery or for accommodating large numbers of wounded, the main function of the ambulance was to patch the men up sufficiently to get them to the Casualty Clearing Stations, which were further back out of range of the enemy artillery.

Private Graham was assessed and then moved to 20 Field Ambulance, and then further back to No. 23 General Hospital. His wounds were serious enough to make him a stretcher case – the walking wounded were directed down a specially signed track to the Casualty Clearing Stations. Graham had his field dressing secured, was loaded onto a motor ambulance and transported to no.4 Clearing Station a further ten miles behind the front line.

Even at this early stage, the Field Ambulances and the Clearing Stations were almost full to capacity, as scores and then hundreds of wounded were being brought in from the front. Once in the safety of the Clearing Station, nurses and orderlies examined and classified each wound. Graham – although in physical and physiological pain would have quickly realised that he had received the much-coveted 'Blighty wound' (a non life-threatening wound that was serious enough to incapacitate the soldier and facilitate a journey home).

The soldiers with more serious wounds were marked for the operating tents where surgeons were already hard at work trying to save the lives or the limbs. Men were patiently laying in rows waiting their turn; some died waiting, some others died on the operating table – either way, they were quickly taken outside to await burial; their stretchers were urgently needed. Army Chaplains were also busy, comforting the badly hurt, helping with first aid or taking dictation from men who waited to send letters home. One himself wrote home of his experience of 1 July:

> *The worst wounded seemed often to feel less pain than those who had slighter wounds. The shock of the shattered limb seemed to destroy the nerves in that part of the body. One lad said to me, 'Oh my leg is so stiff Sir,' and the boy's leg was smashed altogether... But I heard no word of complaints and scarcely a groan.*

Like everywhere else, bombs and shells are fairly indiscriminate and the medical staff and the clergy were not exempt in any way: no fewer than 400 doctors were killed or wounded on the Somme. As the battle raged on there was the horrifying thought that the Army may run out of skilled personnel. As the Border Regiment Diary suggested, there was a swift losing of momentum and at 8:30am, a review of the confused situation took place by Generals who were not at the front and not in possession of the whole information. Everyone knew that things had not gone to plan, but what no one knew was that there were almost 30,000 infantrymen killed or wounded in just 60 minutes. One German soldier later wrote of his experiences from the other side of the battlefield:

> *We heard the mines go up; then it was deathly quiet for a few moments. Then the English came walking, as though they were going to the theatre or as though they were on a parade ground. We felt they were mad. Our orders were given in complete calm and every man took careful aim to avoid wasting ammunition... We just had to load and reload. They*

153

went down in their hundreds. You didn't have to aim, you just fired into them. If only they had run, they would have overwhelmed us.

But still the Generals pressed on, continuing the slaughter throughout the day. Rawlinson thought of calling off the attack but his superior, Haig, demanded the assault continue. By mid-morning men were either, pinned down, dead, wounded or trapped. Willie Graham was well out of the carnage by this time – in pain but alive and destined for home. By the end of the day, he was one of 570 casualties – dead or wounded – from the 1st Battalion the Border Regiment; 570 out of 750. Many had survived the carnage of Gallipoli; Lt Fraser, for instance, who was awarded a Distinguished Service Order award while fighting with Sergeant Jim Curran at Turkey Trench at Gallipoli, was heartbreakingly killed at the Somme.

This was representative of every other battalion and every other regiment. In total, 57,470 officers and men had fallen or were missing; of these, over 19,000 were killed or died of wounds. Sixty per cent of all officers involved on the first day were killed. It was the worst day in British military history. But even at this stage, the Generals had no idea of the magnitude of the losses: in his diary, Rawlinson wrote at 7:30pm, 'Casualties to date, 16,000.

Back in Britain, the population had no idea of the catastrophe. Initial reports were actually misleadingly optimistic about the achievements of the allies. One newspaper wrote:

The attack today went well. Our troops swept across the enemy's front trenches... and so, on the first day of the battle, we can say it has been a good day for England and France, it is a day of promise in this war.

This was reflected in the *Cumberland News*

THE GREAT BATTLE OF THE SOMME
A successful British bombardment took place in the Somme Sector over the last weekend as part of a great offensive. Enemy lines were shelled and an important advance was made by our brave men who took part in dashing raids. At one point it was reported that the men were marching through curtains of fire.

The editor of *The Times* went further:

We must express both to General Haig and to the War Office the thanks of the public for the steady stream of news which has been permitted to flow since the battle began. For the first time since the outbreak of the war our people are able to watch in spirit the exploits of their countrymen.

The Allied dead were not referred to in early reports and the first images of wounded were accompanied by optimistic captions. These jingoistic headlines temporarily delayed the accuracy and the extent of British casualties. With wounded men still trapped in No Man's Land, fighting resumed on 2 July and Haig wrote:

> The principle of which we should act is clear. Under no circumstances would it be possible to relax our efforts in this battle without prejudic-ing – probably fatally – the offensive of our allies and their hopes of our victory. We must and we can maintain our offensive.

But as the early days of July passed, it became clear how disastrous that fateful Saturday had been. Each day the newspapers began to teach the people back home the grim realities of war. Endless pictures of young men in uniform peered out from the pages of the newspapers. The magnitude of the slaughter was incomprehensible, even to the Generals who appear to have carried on in a kind of unfeeling trance – blind to the futility and deluded by the objectives (whatever the cost) of the operation.

During these same days, two men were racing back to England from France with metal containers of film that would prove every bit as explosive as the shells that continued in the opposite direction. Geoffrey Malins and John McDowell were official British cinematographers. They were on hand in July 1916 to make what became (and remains to this day) one of the most suc-cessful British films ever made.

To this point, the British public had been subjected to (many inaccurate) highly-coloured reports of German-inflicted atrocities. (Whereas there is little doubt that many atrocities did occur during the war, it is now generally accept-ed that the allies committed as many as the Germans.) Malins and McDowell's *The Battle of the Somme* was intended to be a patriotic propaganda documen-tary; the film ended up giving a very graphic portrayal of trench warfare, showing dead and dying British soldiers. Filming began some days earlier as the troops were billeted behind the lines. Seen today, there is an innocence about the black and white flickering images of these ordinary men smiling awkwardly at the newfangled cameras; the troops are then seen moving towards the front, with actions as far removed from the swagger and marching of subsequent war films as could be imagined.

Some of the scenes of troops going 'over the top' were staged days before the battle actually started, but the film makers did capture many images of the battle itself, including the incredible image of the detonation of the massive mine beneath Hawthorn Ridge Redoubt which signalled the start of the

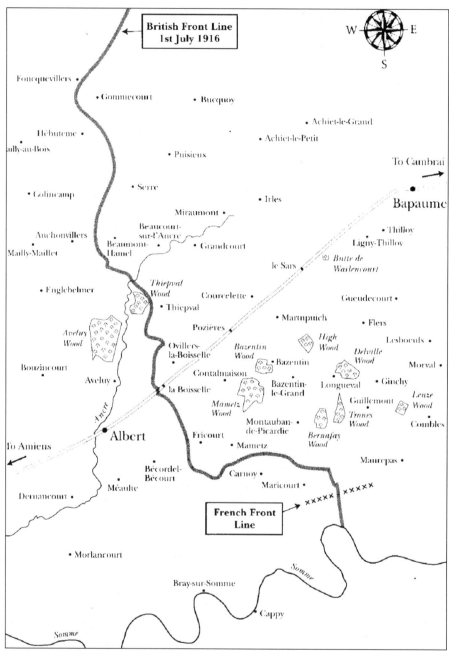

The Battlefield of the Somme (map courtesy of HarperCollins Publishers Ltd.,
© 2005, Richard Holmes)

advance of the 29th Division of the Fourth Army which included Private Graham and 1st Border.

Malins and McDowell were not the only ones to be travelling back across the Channel of course – they were accompanied by thousands of wounded British soldiers; among their number was Willie Graham. As the battle raged on, he left the British Expeditionary Force at Etaples, spent the night in The Eight Apples Hospital near Boulogne and was then shipped to Brighton as early at 9 July 1916 – just over a week after being wounded on the first day. Once in Brighton he was assessed, classified and quickly moved out – his destination was the Royal Army Medical Corps 2nd Northern General hospital at Preston where he remained for the next six weeks.

What he had left in France was an utter debacle: refusing to accept defeat, General Haig continued the slaughter on the Somme, and it went on for a further four months. Geoffrey Malins meanwhile was editing his and his colleague's film in London preparing to show the first day's insanity. He and McDowell had not set out to make a long film, but once the volume and quality of their footage had been seen upon their return, it was decided to compile a feature-length film. Once edited, it lasted ten seconds short of 63 minutes; on 10 August 1916 – while the battle raged on a hundred miles south across the Channel – the film received its first public screening at The Scala Theatre in London.

Less than a week later, the film began showing simultaneously in 34 London cinemas, as word spread of its explosive content; a week later, it found its way into towns and cities around the country. The general public were both thrilled and horrified by what they saw: some considered a vital morale-boosting exercise to see how 'our boys' are doing (very badly as it turned out). While some were talking about morale, others were protesting about morals, considering it in poor taste to glorify in war and bereavement.

Whether for or against, the British public flocked to see the film in their droves. An estimated 20 million tickets were purchased in the film's first two months – it was a cruel irony that thousands upon thousands of soldiers were queuing up to be sent over the top, while back home, thousands upon thousands of people were queuing up to watch them.

Willie Graham was finally given a ten-day furlough on 31 August 1916 – he returned to Carlisle for the first time since March, having experienced the horrors of the front in the meantime. There is no record – anecdotal or otherwise – as to how these ten days went; Emma had been holding the domestic fort with their four children while Willie had been away. The returning soldier – wounded or not – can be a sullen creature, reflecting on his recent past and trying to adjust to civilian life, amongst people he can't relate to, and who can't relate to him or his experiences. Willie Graham was known to be a difficult character at the best of times – we can only assume this leave of absence must have been tense and difficult. He returned to Preston on 9 September, where he remained until Monday, 18 September, when he was posted to Biggin Bank army barracks just outside the town to continue his rehabilitation.

On the same day, *The Battle of the Somme* opened in Carlisle; it was shown only yards from Willie's home at the Palace Theatre on Botchergate. The Carlisle audience was gripped like everyone else by what they saw – the silent movie somehow giving the feature an unreal quality, and yet the titles left nothing to the imagination, giving forthright descriptions of death and injury. Within three months almost half of Britain's population had seen it. The film was then sent abroad to eighteen countries. Bizarrely the surviving soldiers themselves saw the film when they were given leave from the front in France. Their main complaint was that because it was a silent film, the dreadful, incessant noise of battle could not be properly conveyed to the viewer. Presumably the fact that they could see it at all – unlike tens of thousands of their colleagues – gave them some consolation.

One of the walking wounded – Private W G Graham of the Border Regiment – was now safely back home in England. If he was intending to settle down to see out the end of the war in quiet anonymity, he had a strange idea as how this could be achieved. Before he left for France, he had got himself into trouble on more than one occasion; now, within six weeks of his new posting, he was at it again. On 29 October 1916 he was found guilty of breaking out of barracks Whilst On Active Duty (WOAS were four letters Willie became very familiar with over the next two years). Missing for eighteen hours, he forfeited one day's pay and was Confined to Barracks (or CB – more familiarity here) for five days. Clearly not put off by this punishment he was absent from afternoon parade on 19 November WOAS – another three days' CB.

The day before this latest misdemeanour (18 November), The Battle of the Somme finally ended – grinding to a pitiful halt. It had lasted over fourteen weeks; the allies had gained a pitiful 125 square miles of bloody mud from the Germans at a cost of 600,000 men: 400,000 British Imperial, and 200,000 French casualties. The Germans suffered 450,000 casualties.

In the satirical 1990s comedy *Blackadder Goes Forth,* actor Stephen Fry plays General Melchet, the elderly, rosy-checked buffoon, with the handle-bar moustache, the Old Etonian hair-do and a complete lack of understanding or care for his subordinates. For us of course, this caricature of the First World

War General that has been formulated in our minds for generations is hilarious. But in 1916, when thousands upon thousands of men were being slaughtered, satire held its tongue.

The terrible human cost of this catastrophe was inescapable and unrest at home was growing. Enthusiasm for the war was well and truly on the wane, conscription had been introduced in January 1916, to supply more troops for front-line service – the people of Britain had now seen what these troops were going to. As morale flagged on the home front, the old spirit of unity began to give way to anger and revolt; protests against conscription; munitions workers threatening to halt the production of shells; unofficial strikes all compounded the government's problems.

On 7 December, the ambitious David Lloyd George succeeded the hapless Herbert Asquith as Prime Minister. (History could have been so different if Lloyd George had accompanied Kitchener on the fateful diplomatic trip to Russia in May 1916, as he was due to do. It transpired that Lloyd George was otherwise engaged with his new Munitions Ministry, so it was decided to send Kitchener alone). The new Prime Minister wasted no time in getting stuck into his generals: not only accusing them of professional incompetence and ignorance, but of personal cowardice (the last point being unfair as fifty eight generals were killed or died of wounds received). Lloyd George reserved his most stinging criticism for Douglas Haig himself, for whom he was openly mistrustful. 'He is brilliant to the top of his Army boots,' he sneered.

He also took personal control of issues at home: as the unrest grew, the Lloyd George knew the government could not afford confrontation with the industrial workers, on whose loyalty they depended. He himself made a direct intervention during a strike in Wales by the coal miners. Carlisle too did not escape the unrest. Thoughts were beginning to turn to life after the war, with a potential shortage of jobs and houses. A near-riot broke out in Willie's old stamping ground of Wapping when a [refugee] Belgian family were evicted from their temporary home. The local clergymen (presumably representing the landlord) was stoned and jeered as he served notice to the family. The Carlisle Tenants Defence League were outraged:

The Carlisle Landlords are always ready to invoke the law when it suited their purpose, but are going outside the law to put up rents and threatening to evict tenants if they dared to resist.

Willie meanwhile had his own issues. He ended the most eventful year of his life with another black mark. 'On 18 December WOAS overstayed his furlough – fifteen days' detention and forfeit fifteen days' pay.'

159

9

One of Life's Survivors

AS 1916 drew to a close, in an effort to increase food volumes, local authorities were given powers to take over unoccupied land for allotments with or without the owner's consent. Throughout the following spring common land, parks and playing fields were dug up and planted. As well as areas like the Bog Field in Wapping that had always been an area for allotments, the beautiful Victoria Park and Bitts Park in the centre of Carlisle found they had to make their own sacrifices for the war effort.

King George V was also keen to set an example as he decreed that potatoes, cabbages and other vegetables should replace geraniums in the flowerbeds opposite Buckingham Palace and in the Royal parks. One family that probably benefited from the local edict was the Grahams of Crown Street. Poor Emma had – like all of her peers – tried to make do and mend on the modest income provided by the authorities while her husband was away at the war. Now he was back, that income was reduced and any spare money Willie was making was either going down his neck or being forfeited. Emma actually found herself worse off when he was home than when he was away.

His first transgression of the New Year came on 17 February 1917 when he was twenty minutes late for the daily parade (three days' CB). Private Graham was then transferred to Crosby on Merseyside but the change of location didn't bring with it a change of attitude. Within a week of his new posting – not content with being late for the daily parade – he was absent altogether on 11 March. Missing for twelve hours, Graham was apprehended by the Military Police on Preston Station at 10am and was given eight days' CB and forfeited six days' pay.

Such incidents, of course, were a complete irrelevance nationally and internationally as the war continued abroad and unrest grew at home. The pre-war dissatisfaction had returned and many looked for an outlet to cleanse their feeling of hardship and grievances. Streets became a powder-keg as anger was at first focused on the German community in Britain, with a series of anti German riots. Thousands of butchers and bakers shops, run by those of

160

German descent were attacked and looted by the poor.

The strain of war was leading to strikes, mutinies and political radicalisation. In Russia, similar pressures triggered the revolution, the Tsarist monarchy was overthrown and the Tsar and his family, taken into custody. Nicholas II was King George V's cousin and close personal friend and he appealed to George for refuge. But for George to offer him safe haven risked stoking the fires of social unrest in Britain – he might even risk his own crown and family. When war started George was seen as a German; he had kept quiet about his courtesy titles of Field Marshall of the Prussian army and Admiral of the Imperial German Navy. Now revolution was in the air and King George was terrified of being associated with a man labelled tyrant by revolutionaries, so, under advice, George decided to leave Nicholas (and his family) to their fate and make his own arrangements.

The king was keen to make himself seem more British, and with it, more secure. First on his rebranding agenda was his declaration that he ceased to be a German prince; second was the problematic question of his given name; Saxe-Coburg-Gotha hardly conjured up images of Richmond and Surbiton – more Munich and Berlin. With rumblings outside the palace as to where the King's loyalties lie, George came up with a masterstroke of spin and diplomacy. He changed the family name to Windsor – what was more English than that? He also declared that his children could marry English partners rather than enter into the hitherto arranged marriages with vetted German spouses (although it would be over sixty years before Lady Diana Spencer became the first Englishwoman to marry an heir to the British throne – George's great grandson Prince Charles – in more than 300 years). Overnight, the Royals had been reinvented; out was the quasi-German dynasty, in was the classic English family.

All of a sudden, things were looking up. America – with all her man-power and equipment – added to the optimism by finally entering the war in April. Willie Graham decided to celebrate their entry by going missing from duty and treating himself to a night out in Liverpool. (Well okay – author's discretion! But if the reason was fanciful, his actions were factual). Net result: CB and another sixteen days' pay forfeited. There is no question of Emma sharing our amusement – losing another sixteen shillings was no laughing matter to a downtrodden wife with four kids to feed. She had the opportunity to appeal to her husband personally, later that month.

On 18 April, Willie turned up at home unannounced. Probably unbeknown to Emma, he was absent without leave again. The civil police came knocking at 44 Crown Street at 3.20pm and apprehended Willie, prior to sending him back down to Merseyside where he was fined a further six days' pay. To this point, his long suffering Commanding Officer had been the wonderfully named Lieutenant Colonel Arthur Erskine St Vincent Pollard. Pollard was a decorated career soldier who had served with the Regiment in the Boer War, been CO of the 1st Battalion throughout the Gallipoli campaign, from landing to evacuation, and had been on the Somme himself until 16 July 1916. Wounded, he was now back in Britain as CO of the 3rd Battalion. Perhaps he had looked kindly on Graham – being a fellow wounded Somme veteran – seemingly happy to confine the habitual scallywag to barracks. The latest misdemeanour saw Graham up before Colonel Woodburn, whose powers of punishment were wider.

Picture the scene: the five foot, three inch soldier being quick marched in to the colonel's office between a two-man escort, with burly provost sergeant bellowing in his ear, 'Left-right-left-right-left-right. *Halt!* Left *Turn!* Cap *Orf!'*

The Colonel reads out the charge and then, 'Have you anything to say Graham?'

'Please sir...'

'*HOLD YOUR NOISES!*' screams the provost sergeant from behind.

(That's that then. The army would probably describe it as a fair hearing – although it is difficult to have much sympathy with Willie by this point).

'Field Punishment No. 2 and the forfeit of six days' pay for absence from duty,' announces the colonel.

'*FIELD PUNISHMENT NO. 2 AND FORFEIT OF SIX DAYS' PAY FOR ABSENCE FROM DUTY,*' screams the sergeant, as if no one had heard.

This latest sentence probably did attract Willie's attention however. To date (as well as having his pay docked) he had simply been confined to barracks. CB involved – as King's Regulations put it – performing 'fatigue duties to the fullest possible extent, with a view to relieving well-conducted soldiers there from.' There were also extra parades, including pack drill, under the unforgiving aforementioned Provost Sergeant. One soldier later described what he had witnessed:

> *Seven soldiers in full marching order but without rifles file through a gate and approach a burly figure of a Provost Sergeant, who stands at ease, his silver topped cane under his left arm in the middle of a small field. The straggling party has nearly reached him when suddenly he springs to attention and yells at the nearest man, 'You there, right marker, Halt!'*

and then to the remainder 'Fall in on the left of the marker at the double. Halt. Answer your names.' The Provost Sergeant delivers every order and every homily in a loud hoarse yell, without the least sign of strain or effort and without a pause for either breath or punctuation. There is seldom more than ten paces marched without either a change of direction or formation. 'Into file, right turn. Quick march. On the left form squad. Forward. When you joined the army you joined a body of MEN. If you behave like kids you have to TAKE THE CONSEQUENCES. About turn. By the left. Change direction left. Left form. Forward.'

Fortunately for Willie (only as recently as 1907), flogging in the army had been abolished. The next worst thing however was Field Punishments. Field punishment No. 1. – the more serious – saw a man stood spread-eagled and tied by the ankles and wrists in the form of an X to a 'fixed object', usually a large wheel. The men christened it 'The Crucifixion.' He was obliged to stay in position for several hours every day – 28 days was the most common sentence. Some units even took pleasure in tying the man to the wheel and turning it round every so often until the head is downwards. He could be subjected to 'labour, employment and restraint' as if he was undergoing a sentence of hard labour. Field Punishment No 2 was almost the same, but did not include the daily attachment to a fixed object.

The punishments were designed to maintain discipline in the service but were extremely controversial, even during the war. Many in authority regarded the practice as degrading, primitive and wholly inappropriate for what was essentially a citizen army fighting the war. Whatever the punishment, it didn't seem to prevent Private Graham from trying the patience of his superiors – within six week, he was at it again. He was given a pass to visit home in late May 1917. Due back at the barracks on 26 May, he came rolling in two days late. Another seven days CB and another twelve days pay forfeited. For good measure, as if he didn't give his wife a torrid time financially, during this last visit he left her pregnant.

A week before Willie left Carlisle; his home city was honoured by a visit from the king himself. King George was on a kind of national tour visiting areas that were producing ships and munitions for the war effort. The king visited Barrow before inspected the factory at Gretna. It was a timely morale-boosting visit to the massive works, in what had been a particularly difficult year for the workers there (An idle part of a factory in Silvertown had been pressed into service to a year earlier to manufacture TNT; an explosion there in January 1917 killed 73 and injured 400).

Finally the King and Queen Mary visited Carlisle to review troops. In doing so, he became the first reigning monarch to visit the city since James I (VI of Scotland) in 1617.

Nationally, with the Americans now on board, things were looking far more promising as far as the war was concerned – all of a sudden, it looked as though we might actually win it. Lloyd George certainly thought so and his thoughts were now turning towards the end of the war. There was however still work to be done as far as industrial relations were concerned during the summer of 1917.

The working populace did not share the Prime Minister's upbeat spirit; there was a wave of strikes that summer. War weariness and resentment at profiteering by some, contributed to the discontent but the main reason was the continuing reduction in pay for skilled workers. In some cases, unskilled pay (whether for male or female) came to exceed that given for skilled labour; in addition skilled men were prevented – without obtaining a leaving certificate from the authorities – from leaving one munitions job to seek better pay in another.

The King and Queen arrive in Carlisle (photograph courtesy of Ashley Kendall)

As the year wore on, there developed a food crisis as low wages and spiralling prices were compounded by German submarine blockades which prevented shipping from bringing essential food and materials into Britain. Inevitably the poorest families and communities were hit hardest; malnutrition and poverty were widespread. In 1914 bread was four pence a loaf, in 1917 it was eleven and a half pence; a quart of milk over the same period rose from an average of three and a half to seven and a half pence. And if you were a pregnant mother of four with a wastrel husband who is always either drinking away his pay or getting it docked, it didn't help. For thousands of working class families, the cupboard was well and truly bare.

If they could muster up the energy to list their complaints, after pay and food came housing. The Grahams of Crown Street were typical of a working class family of the day: living in rooms and houses rented from private landlords, struggling to keep a clean and respectable home amid severe overcrowding. Life was made even more difficult by a frequent lack of running water and decent sanitation. Typical also, were the number of children – an average family during the First World War included 4.6 children (Emma had four and one on the way in 1917).

In towns and cities the problems of overcrowding were exacerbated by the influx of refugees and munitions workers; often hostels, schools and church halls were converted to provide a roof for thousands. Barrow was a typical example of housing-related unrest: a significant number of Belgian refugees had been sent to Barrow to work in the shipbuilding yards after fleeing their country at the start of the war. Some of these refugees had, in time, bought houses, subsequently applying for warrants to evict the [local] sitting tenants. Tension simmered on the streets; the authorities – fearing that the shipbuilding effort could be detrimentally affected – designated Barrow a 'special area' in which the building of new, temporary accommodation for workers was urgently undertaken.

The misery of the masses was complete in 1917 when it turned out to be a desperately cold winter. Coal fires were the main source of heating but the price of coal had mirrored that of food since the start of the war and supplies were irregular and often ran out. The cause of the short supply was in no small part to the number of miners who had been conscripted or volunteered, and sent to the front. Shops closed early to save heating and lighting, while families were going to bed earlier for the same reason. A few short years earlier, Willie Graham and his carter colleagues had been involved in a dispute about the moving of coal from Crown Street to Botcherby; this must have seemed very silly and insignificant now.

The Bishop of London wrote a letter to the *Daily Telegraph* in which he stated:

>...*while nine soldiers died every hour in 1915, twelve babies died every hour, so that it was more dangerous to be a baby than a soldier.*

Around one in ten babies died before they reached their first birthday. Whooping cough, diphtheria, scarlet fever, tuberculosis all wreaked havoc with infants in the bed-sharing, overcrowded hovels.

By late 1917, social division on the home front was reaching crisis point. Anti conscription meetings were violently attacked by hard line patriots as the police stood by. Vandalism, rioting and looting were no longer restricted to German shops – any shop was fair game for many of the hungry poor; once someone had cast the first stone and broke a window, things would quickly degenerate into a go-for-broke free-for-all, with everyone wading in and filling their pockets and bags. Some in the government feared that morale was so low that the country was close to collapse. A few believed there might be a revolution similar to that which had ousted the monarchy and the old regime in Russia.

The King reviewing troops at Edenside (photograph courtesy of Ashley Kendall)

Private Graham meanwhile appears to have taken all of this national unrest in his stride. His latest brush with his superiors came on 13 August when he overstayed his pass for 22 hours and fifteen minutes. Seven days CB and another fifteen days' pay forfeited. But what did catch the bold-lad's attention in late 1917 was the thing he must have feared more than anything else – a beer shortage. With the food shortage came a lack of sugar and other raw materials needed for beer production. Production was reduced by government order and pubs were rationed. The decrease in sales meant decrease in profits, so price rises were inevitable. When prices rose to eight pence a pint in Liverpool, the dockers wrecked some pubs and boycotted others, forcing the government to increase beer production by a third. (Whether our Willie was in the background cheering the Dockers on is unknown.)

On the night of 23 November 1917, he had obviously found one oasis on Merseyside to satisfy his needs: he was arrested by the Military Police for being 'Drunk and inappropriately dressed in Mary's Lane, Thornton at 10:15pm.' King's regulations established fines for drunkenness at 2s/6d for the first offense and five shillings for the second, rising to a punitive ten shillings if the offense had been committed within three months of a previous lapse (no prizes for guessing what Willie got). Oh yes, and another seven days in the slammer.

10

The End's in Sight

ON 27 February 1918 the CO of the 3rd Battalion the Border Regiment Lieutenant Colonel Pollard received some good news; in fact at the end of a long and illustrious career in which he had seen several campaigns and served his regiment with distinction on three different continents, this day probably ranked quite highly amongst his most memorable, because on 27 February 1918, Pollard received confirmation that Private Willie Graham was being compulsorily transferred out of his battalion.

William George Graham was fast becoming the Norman Stanley Fletcher of the British Army; he was a habitual offender who accepted arrest and pay deduction as an occupational hazard and presumably accepted imprisonment in the same casual manner. Fortunately for him, he spent very little time at the front during the war; had he done so, the punishments received would have been more severe – even deadly.

He was transferred to the Labour Corps with immediate effect. (There is no record in the Regimental Diary of Pollard throwing a gala event but the poor man must surely have treated himself to a celebratory brandy in a darkened room that night.)

The Labour Corps were basically a group that carried out all kinds of supporting roles, from agricultural work, to managing and escorting Prisoners of War, to road construction. To be designated a place in the Labour Corps, a man usually fell into one of two categories: he was either unfit for front line duties or he was rascal who was more trouble than he was worth in his regiment. Clearly Willie Graham fitted both categories.

Without wishing to waste any unnecessary time, the Border Regiment arranged for the transfer to take place on 28 February – the day after notification was received; Private 21609 Graham of the Border Regiment became Private 662960 of the Labour Corps. Making sure he took nothing of theirs with him, he was ordered to return the following:

1 pair of ankle boots

1 cap

2 pairs drawers
1 pair gloves
2 service dress jackets
1 pair of puttees
2 pairs of service dress trousers
1 cardigan
1 great coat

The following day, his latest son Sidney was born, but almost before Graham was established with his new unit, he found himself in hospital with scabies. Scabies – a contagious skin disease caused by the itch of a mite which burrows under the skin – was another common complaint of the First World One soldier, given that it was an easily contracted disease in the filth and the squalor of the trenches; but strangely in Private Graham's case, he had contracted it having been back in Britain in reasonably hygienic conditions for over eighteen months. The mild dose of the disease kept Willie in hospital for five days and by the end of March, he was with his new colleagues. It wasn't long however before he was up to his old tricks – in May he was found guilty of breaking out of barracks while on active service (WOAS); this resulted in another eight days CB and another day's pay being surrendered.

As the war chugged through its final few months, the country prepared for peace; front-line soldiers prepared to return home – although they did not know what they would be returning to; children, who had only known war-time tried to understand the concept of peace-time with (hopefully) their fathers returning home. Britain would have to be a very different country to the one that went to war to defend four years earlier. The men had been through the mud and hell of Flanders while the women had raised children on a pittance and worked in the factories to help the war effort.

As months to the end of the war became weeks, Willie's life became gradually easier. He was initially posted to Nottingham to perform agricultural work in September; the following month he was transferred to 538 Agricultural Company of the Labour Corps back in Carlisle. No sooner was he back in his home city than he found himself in hospital again; on 19 October he was admitted to Fusehill Hospital suffering with bronchitis. And no sooner was he out of hospital than he was up before the beak again, this time, surpassing even his own previous efforts. On 2 November he was apprehended for being absent from daily parade; not happy with this, Graham broke out of barracks whilst being under open arrest and went missing for the night

– rolling back into barracks (probably the worse for wear) – the following morning. More CB, more pay docked.

The following week on 11 November 1918, the war finally ground to a halt with the signing of the Armistice. After four years, over 8 million dead soldiers and 21 million others wounded, and 25 million additional deaths later, the war was over.

Britain had put together an army the likes of which had never been seen before: over 4 million men went to France and nearly three quarters of a million stayed their forever. Some 300,000 children had lost at least one parent. One in ten of an entire generation of young men had been wiped out and with such loss, tiny hamlets and villages – with no returning men to help sustain them – disappeared too. The Border Regiment was awarded a staggering 64 battle honours during the war and its officers and men won five Victoria Crosses. The price it paid for such glory however was high and representative of many regiments; a total of 7,450 casualties were suffered between 1914 and 1918.

Any thought of rejoicing gave way to exhaustion and sorrow. The celebrated war-time nurse and writer Vera Britain noticed that 'the men and women who looked incredulously into each other's faces did not shout 'we've won the war' they simply said, 'the war is over'.' The country may have won the war; an even bigger challenge now was to win the peace.

During the war the suffragettes had ceased agitation and made notable contributions to many aspects of the war effort; in doing so, they succeeded in finding favour with public opinion. Before 1918 was out, Parliament repaid their efforts and peaceful representation by recognising the skills and intelligence of women by passing the Representation of the People Act: all female householders were enfranchised, as were householders' wives, and women university graduates over 30 years of age. (Bizarrely, if this move was in gratitude for women's war work, it was surely misplaced – why did only women over the age of 30 get the vote while it was mainly the younger women who had done the work? For her peaceful campaign for women's rights Millicent Garrett Fawcett would receive the Grand Cross, Order of the British Empire in 1925).

The now burgeoned electorate also put their faith in Lloyd George in the election of December 1918 – he and his coalition government were returned with a majority of 262 seats. The Prime Minister promised a post-war Britain 'fit for heroes,' but this election was not without controversy either: some Labour politicians complained that the election had been rushed through before many serving soldiers could return to express their views. Nasty innuendoes were aimed at farmers who had stayed at home and made their pile, while their labourers fought and bled on the continent; and firms were criticised for failing to keep their promises of leaving pre-war jobs open for men who left to fight – by the time they came back (*if* they came back) they found the jobs filled by men who did not go to war.

In an attempt to quell the growing social unrest, the government put controls on food prices and guaranteed all families a basic supply of staples like bread, sugar tea and meat. Food supplies from overseas were quickly re-established and lucky stars were thanked as the final year of the war produced a good harvest. At last, the nightmare of hunger and starvation receded but in a cruel twist, the country was hit by a global Spanish flu pandemic and another 150,000 people would be lost over the forthcoming winter.

At the start of the war, Kitchener's call to arms caused an enormous countrywide operation to get men into the army; now at its end the government faced was an equally massive administrative challenge to get them out of it. Returning soldiers destined to return to civilian life were divided into demobilisation groups. The first group was generally pre-war civil servants, and would themselves manage the demobilising of their colleagues. Other groups consisted of 'pivotal men' who would, the government believed, create jobs

Bertram Carr, the mayor of Carlisle, announces the Armistice from the steps of the Town Hall (photograph courtesy of Ashley Kendall)

for others; 'slip men' who had an employer's slip promising a job; men who were expected to find work rapidly; and finally those for whom the process was expected to be more difficult. Not surprisingly, our Willie fell into the final category and had to remain in the army a little longer. Not unnaturally, these men weren't too enamoured with this edict – they had signed to serve for the duration of the war and hankered after freedom now that the fighting was over; why couldn't they just go home? Private Graham would be one of three million men discharged in 1919 (some others would be destined to wait until 1920).

Willie was not the sharpest knife in the box but his unorthodox conduct appears to have led to a relatively early release from the army after all. On 6 January 1919 he went missing from duty for the umpteenth time – for this he was given 96 hours detention and deducted a further six days' pay. Of course Private Graham had previous – and lots of it. It would appear that the British Army decided to cut its losses with this latest transgression as he was given notice to demobilise before the month was out. On 25 January he completed his papers, was given a medical category as A1(!) and signed a form headed 'I DO NOT CLAIM TO BE SUFFERING FROM A DISABILITY DUE TO MY MILITARY SERVICE.' It can only be assumed that both parties must have been delighted with the outcome.

As he and thousands like him arrived home, the spin of officialdom went into overdrive – homes fit for heroes were promised, where families could settle down into prosperous domestic bliss. But then, as now, real life never quite lived up to officialdom's propaganda. Before terms like post traumatic stress disorder were ever invented, traumatised war veterans found it difficult to fit into home life at all; unemployment rose rapidly with the masses of soldiers now in civvie-street and the old chestnut of women doing men's work inevitably reared its head again.

It was every man (or woman) for themselves as females too were divided, with single and widowed women claiming a prior right to employment over married women. One lady reflected a widely held view in a letter to the *Daily Herald* in October 1919:

> *No decent man would allow his wife to work, and no decent woman would do it if she knew the harm she was doing to the widows and single girls who are looking for work. Put the married women out, send them home to clean their houses and look after the man they married and give a mother's care to their children. Give the single women and widows the work.*

It was clear that adjusting to a post-war routine was not proving easy for anyone – absent soldiers had missed their families growing up and wives and children had to get used to having a man about the house again. Emma Graham and her children typified the hardship endured by those at home during the First World War; the hunger and unrest suffered by millions like the Grahams will always be overshadowed by the far great suffering and death endured by the soldiers at the front, but his still one of the forgotten stories of British history. It may have been a subsequent overstatement to say a whole generation was lost, but it certainly isn't to claim a whole generation was traumatised – at home and abroad – by the horrors of the war.

Notwithstanding the flu pandemic, the eighteen months immediately after the war appeared to be making good on Lloyd George's promises. The country experienced an economic boom and the Housing and Planning Act placed a statutory responsibility on local authorities to provide homes for a weekly

Willie and some of his children in Crown Street c1924

rent. The building of some 200,000 homes across the country began; this was effectively the beginning of council house construction that would continue throughout the remainder of the twentieth century. In Carlisle, the Act would be the catalyst for the development of council estates in Harraby, Upperby, Currock, Botcherby, Raffles, Belah and Denton Holme – over the following twenty years tenants would be taken from slum clearance areas closer to the city centre and re-housed in the new properties.

Other post-war reforms included the raising the school leaving age to fourteen, standardising salaries, increasing old age pensions, and extending unemployment insurance. But, as with everything, when something seems too good to be true – it normally is. Boom quickly turned to bust as 1920 turned into 1921 and many fat-cat employers treated their employees like dogs by adopting draconian pre-war methods of wage cuts and lock-outs. Upon his return to normality, Willie resumed his two main interests in life: between 1920 and 1933, Emma had another six children; she also experienced the horrors of infant mortality when one of the twins she bore was lost (my grandmother's theory was that had it not been for the war, she would have probably had two more children).

How much this pastime was linked to his other pursuit will never probably be known, but the sinister spectre of the worse-for-wear husband returning late from the pub loomed large at 44 Crown Street. So much so that his wife regularly asked one of her eldest children to stay up with her until he was home and settled in bed, thus avoiding any unpleasantries that would never occur in the sacrosanct presence of the children.

The Currock Estate c1934 (photograph courtesy of Ashley Kendall)

In Willie's absence, of course, the pubs and breweries had been compulsorily purchased as part of the State Management Scheme. Carlisle had been such a successful pilot for the scheme, it was extended to several other areas throughout the country; but as the government ceased the schemes in most of the other areas, they decided to keep the scheme in Carlisle in an effort to control alcohol abuse. (Whether Willie's impending return had any influence on this decision is mere speculation.)

Along with the scheme came the re-branding on your average public house; Carlisle's pubs gradually saw refurbishment and architectural indulgence that would be copied throughout the country. (Many pubs were the work of the architect Harry Redfern, after whom a pub was named later). At first the parochial Carliseans took exception to government's decision to continue its control of the liquor trade; Willie remained ambivalent – who cares about Harry and his fancy designs, or where the liquor comes form, it all goes down the same way.

His favourite haunts were naturally The Crown at the end of the street and The Irish Gate near the castle. His usual routine on a Saturday evening was to leave the Irish Gate at closing time (10pm) and visit the green market close by that was open to 11pm where he got a cheap lump of meat that hadn't been sold that day, for Sunday dinner.

If Willie was a man of his generation, then Emma was certainly a woman of hers, making do and mending for her burgeoning family, and seemingly producing meals for all when no food appeared to exist. 'A lot of home made bread and tatty pots,' one of her sons recalls today, 'she was a good cook and baker.'

To his credit, Willie was renowned as a good gardener and the vegetables from his allotment would be put to good use by the woman of the house. One strange characteristic about Emma was that she never liked flowers and would not have them in the house; Willie therefore relied on his entrepreneurial skills by growing flowers on his patch and selling them to neighbours. (More money for you-know-what.)

Upon his return from the war, he managed to revert to his old trade, albeit as a Coal Horse and Cart-man for the Corporation – his job was simply to deliver coal around the city. But it wasn't long before officialdom was on his tail again, chasing him up for documents he should have returned upon his leaving the army. In classic Willie-style, he appears to have ignored the correspondence and it was left to the long-suffering and gentle Emma to reply on his behalf:

Dear Sir

In answer to your letter dated 30 October 1919, I am writing to state my husband was out of the Army and has been since the latter end of January this year. He has nothing now belonging to the Army and I hope this is all you need to know.

I will remain yours truly

Signed Mrs. E Graham,
44 Crown Street, Carlisle.

There remained one last army-related experience. In March 1922, Willie received his campaign medals from the Record Office in Nottingham: the British War Medal and the Victory Medal acted as the final reminders of his military service.

11

Postscript

THE war altered the whole political landscape of Europe; prior to it, there had been six continental Emperors within seven years King George V was the only one left, and even he had lost a considerable portion of his Empire. Perhaps the greatest barometer of change came in 1924 when Ramsey MacDonald became Britain's first Labour Prime Minister – the party was barely twenty years old and yet the working populace had made their feelings known and the old political landscape was changed forever.

In 1928 women received equal suffrage with men when their voting age was lowered to the age of 21 (a year later trade union leader Margaret Bondfield became the first woman cabinet member in British history).

The redevelopment of Carlisle continued but signalled the death knell for the area of Wapping. Houses were demolished and families were moved to other areas of the city. The Grahams moved into one of the new council houses on Millholme Avenue at Currock – ten shillings per week for the three-bedroomed property with its own facilities was a veritable luxury when compared with the one-up-one-down house on Crown Street. With the new location came a new local for Willie Graham – The Currock on Boundary Road would see a lot of his custom over the next few years. He also secured an allotment on Upperby Road that would serve Emma well as she continued to concoct meals for her brood out of very little.

As far as work was concerned, Willie could never be accused of slacking – he was always looking for work – and usually found something to keep him going; from carter to cleaner, to labourer to doorman. One of his favourite jobs came when he landed a job at the Palace Cinema on Botchergate. Free films, light work and a chance to nip out to the Golden Lion at St Nicholas when the boss wasn't looking. When coming out of work one night, Willie had the misfortune of being knocked over on busy Botchergate which had gradually seen a significant increase in motor cars. Typical Willie – he turned misfortune on its head by successfully claiming significant compensation from the accident. No doubt he would regale his drinking partners with the sequence of events that brought drinks all round. One of Willie's other favourite scams was to run a sweep in the Irish Gate Pub; this was an illegal (but common) practice, that saw the patrons betting on various things from horses to two flies climbing up a wall. One of Willie's sons remembers how he won the sweep being run by his Dad one night, when he wasn't even in the pub!

If such Del-Boy-type-fiddles were amusing – as has been suggested earlier – there was a more sinister side to Willie Graham and one of the less funnier incidents came in the late 1940s. Before the Second World War one of the affluent Ridley family died. The Ridleys were the family who Emma's mother worked for over 50 years earlier and had had an affair with one of the boys. To his credit, Ridley never forgot his unknown child and upon his death, he made arrangements in his will to see his biological daughter financially recognised.

The unusual sight of two suited solicitors knocking at 43 Millholme Avenue, Carlisle caused a bit of a stir amongst the locals. The man of the house was at work when the news they delivered to Emma Graham was that she had inherited a four-figure sum. The modestly educated mother of eleven asked her sons for guidance – they encouraged her not to sign any documentation at this stage but to take some time to reflect before any major decisions were made. All that changed, however, when Willie got home with pound signs in his eyes. He pressured his wife to signing whatever documentation would release the money – he then helped her spend it by helping the profits of the State Management Scheme and – much to the disgust of his own son –

Willie and Emma c1960

acting the 'big man' by treating minor acquaintances to presents of pipes and tobacco. Emma's inheritance disappeared in a matter of weeks.

And so his life continued: the cyclical pattern of job, home, Friday and Saturday nights in the pub, Sunday lunchtime in the pub – back home for lunch and afternoon sleep – and back out on Sunday nights. Emma's routine included trying to intercept him on a Friday night at the door of the pub to rescue some of the weekly wage. Other expedients

Emma with great-grandchildren Mark, Martin and Anne circa 1968.

included pawning her rings on a Monday and recovering the valuables on a Friday; and borrowing the rent money from her son-in-law. (The son-in-law in question was Neil Curran – one of Jim Curran's sons. Neil married Bell Graham, in 1935. They were the author's grandparents).

Willie Graham died in 1967, aged 81. It may seem a bit mean to short change him by whizzing through the last forty or so years of his life, but events like the Great Depression of the 1930s and the Second World War, and the effect they had on the masses, will be covered another time; and besides – it is probably not best to delve too deeply into the life of this particular ancestor. He and Jim Curran personify the lives of millions of ordinary men of their generation. Willie Graham – with all his faults and foibles – was representative of many a working class patriarch of the early twentieth century. Anyone thinking about embarking on their own mission to discover their heritage should be warned that you cannot view all of your family history through rose coloured glasses – like it or not, there are many Willie Grahams in all our histories.

Emma outlasted him by three years and his beloved State Management Scheme outlasted him by four. When the government announced the sell-off of the brewery and pubs, most local drinkers were devastated; their fathers and grandfathers had been against the scheme in 1917 but they had grown up to appreciate the tasty brew of 'State Management,' as well as Carlisle's own

179

whiskey, 'Border Blend.' In 1921, official reports referred to the scheme as 'an experiment'; lasting over fifty years it turned out to be the longest running experiment in British political history.

Principal Sources

Bibliography

Barnett, Correlli, *The Great War,* BBC, 2003

Bilton, David, *The Home Front in the Great War,* Leo Cooper, 2003

Cecil, Robert, *Life in Edwardian England,* B.T. Batsford Ltd, 1969

Davies, Norman, *The Isles, A History*, Macmillan, 1999

Ferguson, Niall, *Empire: How Britain Made the Modern World*, Allen Lane, 2003

Grigg, John, *Lloyd George – War Leader*, Allen Lane, 2002

Holmes, Richard, *Tommy,* Harper Collins, 2004

Humphries, Steve and Van Emden, Richard, *All Quiet on the Home Front,* Headline, 2003

Van Emden, Richard and James, Lawrence, *The Rise and Fall of the British Empire,* Abacus, 1998

Jenkins, Roy, *Churchill,* Pan Books, 2002

May, Ralph, *Glory Is No Compensation,* The Border Regiment and King's Own Royal Border Regiment Museum, 2003

Middlebrook, Martin, *The First Day On The Somme - 1 July 1916,* Penguin, 1984

Moorehead, Alan, *Gallipoli,* Wordsworth Ed Ltd, 1997

Petrie, Sir Charles, *Scenes from Edwardian England,* Eyre & Spottiswoode, 1965

Rollinson, William, *The History of Cumberland and Westmorland,* Phillimore & Co, 1978

Schama, Simon, *A History of Britain Vol III,* BBC Worldwide, Ltd, 2002

Starkey, David, *Monarchy,* Harper Perennial, 2007

Sutherland, Douglas, *Tried and Valliant,* Lee Cooper Ltd, 1972

Towill, Sydney, *Church and State in the Diocese of Carlisle,* Sydney Towill, 2000

Towill, Sydney, *Georgian and Victorian Carlisle,* Carnegie Publishing, 1996

Articles and Public Reports
Carlisle City Council City Minutes, 1875-1939
Power, W H, *Report on the Local Government Board on Recent Epidemic Prevalence of Fever in Carlisle, and the Sanitary State of the City*, 1874

Newspapers & Magazines
Carlisle Journal
Carlisle Patriot
Cumberland Paquet
Cumberland News
Daily Telegraph
The Times
The *Regiment Magazine*, Issue Eight

Records & Private Papers
Church Records of St Bede's, Carlisle 1880-1915
Papers belonging to the Border and King's Own Royal Border Regiment (including the regimental diaries from the Boer War and the Great War)
School Log, St Bede's School, Carlisle 1890-1905
Service Records of Private William George Graham (Public Records Office)
Service Records of Sergeant James Curran (Public Records Office)

Web sites
BBC History
Carlisle History
Channel 4 History
First World War.com
Genuki
National Army Museum
The Imperial War Museum
The War Times Journal
Public Records Office

By the same author

Non Fiction:

Glory Boy! (2000)
The Carlisle Floods: One Story (2005)
For Queen and Cumberland (2008)

Fiction:
Sherlock Holmes and the Carlisle Adventure of the Spanish Drums (2003)